Confidence Restored

The History of The Tenth District's Federal Reserve Bank

GRAHAM, ANDERSON, PROBST & WHITE ARCHTS.

✸ FEDERAL RESERVE BANK OF KANSAS CITY ✸

In the early years, messengers played an important role in the Federal Reserve Bank of Kansas City's operations. Messengers and the Bank security guards also wore distinct uniforms.

Confidence Restored

THE HISTORY *of* THE TENTH DISTRICT'S FEDERAL RESERVE BANK

PUBLISHED BY THE PUBLIC AFFAIRS DEPARTMENT *of* THE FEDERAL RESERVE BANK *of* KANSAS CITY

1 MEMORIAL DRIVE • KANSAS CITY, MO 64198

Diane M. Raley, publisher

Lowell C. Jones, executive editor

Tim Todd, author

Casey McKinley, designer

Cindy Edwards, archivist

Edited by: Sara Brunsvold and Brye Steeves

Special thanks to: Amy Williams, deputy director,
                    Harry S. Truman Presidential Library *&* Museum

                    Mary Beveridge, manager,
                    Missouri Valley Special Collections, Kansas City Public Library

First Edition

ISBN 0-9744809-2-4

Contents

Foreword

Kansas City is the regional headquarters for the central bank of the United States' Tenth Federal Reserve District.

The Bank's history is a story with which you are likely unfamiliar. The occasion of our move to a new headquarters building prompted us to carefully review our well-assembled but little-used archives. One of the results is the volume you now hold. This book tells many stories revolving around a few key events. The first is a nation recognizing that its financial success is determined not only by the major cities on its coasts, but involves the entire country, which is reflected in this great system called the Federal Reserve. The others are the successful local efforts that were crucial when decisions were made about where the Bank and its Branches would be located.

We are pleased that our Bank's story is also the story of the bankers, businessmen, farmers and laborers who make up the economy in Missouri, Kansas, Nebraska, Colorado, Oklahoma, Wyoming and New Mexico – the region that we are proud to serve as the Tenth Federal Reserve District.

The Federal Reserve Bank of Kansas City performs some unique functions as the central bank. We participate in the conduct of monetary policy, help ensure safety and soundness in the banking system, and provide financial services to commercial banks and the United States Treasury.

Each of our mission areas could certainly merit an extensive history of its own. However, at its core, the story of any institution is a story of its people. In this history you will not find a detailed account of Federal Reserve policy or regulatory actions, but you will discover the stories of the individuals who established the Federal Reserve in Kansas City. Some of the names you will recognize, while others may be largely unknown. They are not exclusively Kansas Citians, coming instead from the large area that the city serves as a regional hub.

It is appropriate that a regionwide effort led to the founding of the Bank and its Branches in Denver, Oklahoma City and Omaha. Our ties to the communities we serve are a vital component of the Federal Reserve's structure today. Residents from across the Tenth District serve crucial roles as directors and advisory council members, offering their input on economic and banking issues. These individuals are a very literal link between our communities and the central bank's policy deliberations. They tie the Federal Reserve to the nation's Main Streets, preventing it from becoming an isolated, and insulated, Washington-based institution.

I want to thank those individuals who played a major role in bringing this book to completion. I particularly want to thank Diane Raley, vice president and public information officer, who created this book and shepherded it to completion. I also want to recognize Tim Todd, assistant manager in Public Affairs, who did most of the research and authored the text; Cindy Edwards, archivist, who provided much of the material contained within the covers of this book; and Casey McKinley, graphic designer, who combined their efforts in this volume.

We believe sharing this history will help both our Bank employees as well as those we serve better understand our past in order to be better prepared for our future.

Thomas M. Hoenig, President
Federal Reserve Bank of Kansas City

Introduction

Some may be surprised to learn that the Federal Reserve is the nation's third central bank.

The first Bank of the United States, designed by Treasury Secretary Alexander Hamilton, was established in 1791 in what was then the nation's capital of Philadelphia. The Bank, created to help the country handle debt from the Revolutionary War and standardize currency, was controversial from the start. Some protested its constitutionality, and many were fearful of its influence. When it came time to renew the Bank's 20-year charter, its critics were able to generate enough support in a Congress that was almost evenly divided on the issue, and the renewal failed by a single vote in both houses.

Only a few years later, however, lawmakers found themselves once again discussing the idea of a central bank. After the War of 1812, Congress quickly realized that it needed a way to regulate banking and credit as well as stabilize the nation's currency. The Second Bank of the United States was chartered under President James Madison in 1816. Like its predecessor, the Second Bank was plagued by public distrust and became a target for the populist President Andrew Jackson, who made the Bank one of the key issues in his re-election campaign. After a particularly bitter fight between Jackson and the head of the Second Bank, the bank's charter was not renewed.

Neither the first nor second central banks of the United States were widely understood by the public at

large. Although the banks had branch offices throughout the country, there was much concern about the perceived connections to the business and banking powers in the Northeast. Especially suspicious were those living in rural areas of the South and along the nation's frontier who not only felt disconnected from the eastern cities, but also distrustful of the power they believed was held by bankers in that part of the country.

The years following the demise of the second bank saw the U.S. economy endure a number of financial panics as commercial banks across the country suffered serious liquidity problems, business credit collapsed and the public suffered severe financial hardship. After the Panic of 1907, Congress recognized that the nation needed economic and financial stability and began the discussions that led to the third central bank.

The Federal Reserve

Aware of history, lawmakers knew that one of the first and most important challenges they faced was determining the new bank's structure. In his memoirs, Paul Warburg, one of the founders of the Federal Reserve, notes that two of the main objections to the creation of a central bank were the danger

Local bankers were the guests at a dinner celebrating the opening of the Bank's headquarters at 925 Grand on Nov. 16, 1921. Federal Reserve Gov. W.P.G. Harding was the guest of honor at the event held at Kansas City's Muehlebach Hotel.

of political control and the danger of control by special interests. Clearly, history had shown that a highly centralized bank with concentrated authority, while perhaps successful in other nations, would not work in the United States, where the distribution of power and authority are the central component in its form of government.

Facing these challenges, congressional leaders, including Oklahoma Sen. Robert L. Owen, created a new structure. It would be a network of regional banks, each operating under the leadership of local boards of directors, with oversight by a government agency, the Board of Governors of the Federal Reserve System, in Washington, D.C.

It was a unique combination – a "decentralized" central bank that blends both public and private control in a reflection of the nation's checks and balances system. It is accountable to, yet independent of, the government.

The founders recognized that this network of regional banks was an essential element in building and maintaining trust in the institution. The bank's long-term success required a structure sharing responsibility and power across the country instead of confining them within the government or along Wall Street. And communities across the nation were eager to play their part.

Determination &

THE FEDERAL RESERVE

Achievement

BANK *of* KANSAS CITY

The building AT 1 MEMORIAL DRIVE
is a testament TO THE DETERMINATION OF KANSAS CITY.

When President Woodrow Wilson signed the Federal Reserve Act on Dec. 23, 1913, many cities launched campaigns to win one of the regional offices of the nation's new "decentralized" central bank.

There were some clear favorites.

New York, Chicago, Pittsburgh, Boston and St. Louis were deemed "practically certain to be chosen" by *The New York Times* in its Dec. 24, 1913 edition. The paper rounded out its list of likely choices with Philadelphia; New Orleans; San Francisco; Portland; St. Paul; Washington, D.C.; and Louisville.

Kansas City?

Its only mention in the article came in a list ranking cities by the amount of capital and surplus held in their national banks, where it finished a lackluster 18th.

Eastern cities that viewed themselves as the most appropriate locations were critical of Kansas City. Perhaps most troubling of all, even Missouri's own senators appeared to have limited interest in the idea of a Kansas City Federal Reserve Bank.

"There was prevalent … a feeling throughout the country that Kansas City would not get one of the Banks," Jess Worley wrote in an unpublished Bank history authored in the early 1920s. "So strong was this feeling … repeated to the ears of Kansas Citians that a spirit of keen determination took hold of Kansas City bankers."

A *competitive fire* HAD BEEN STOKED.

A New Type *of* Central Bank

The Federal Reserve Act created a central bank comprising a unique network of Banks serving local regions, or Federal Reserve Districts, with national coordination by a Board of Governors[1] in Washington, D.C. But when it came to locating the regional Banks, both the cities where they would operate and the regions they would serve, the Act devoted only about 300 words – essentially a lengthy paragraph that made just a few key requirements:

- There would be between eight and 12 Federal Reserve Districts.
- The Districts would "be apportioned with due regard to the convenience and customary course of business."
- A Reserve Bank Organizing Committee, comprising the Secretary of the Treasury, the Secretary of Agriculture and the Comptroller of the Currency, would create the Districts and designate "Federal Reserve cities" where the regional Banks would be located.
- The Act gave the Committee a deadline to complete their work "as soon as practicable."

To sign the Act, Wilson delayed his departure for a Gulf Coast vacation for several days while Congress worked to approve the legislation. A similar urgency was exhibited by the Reserve Bank Organizing Committee. With Wilson still considering nominees for Comptroller of the Currency, the Committee was a two-member panel, but it quickly forged ahead with Agriculture Secretary David F. Houston and Treasury Secretary William G. McAdoo holding their first informal meeting on Christmas Day in McAdoo's home near Washington's Dupont Circle. The Committee's first formal session was held the following day at the Treasury.

"We do not propose to let any grass grow under the feet of the organization Committee," McAdoo told a reporter. "We are going at these problems carefully but quickly."

The pressure to complete their task quickly only compounded the already difficult question of how to divide the country.

"Nothing had aroused such scorn and ridicule, nothing had been so fiercely fought in Congress, nothing had so generally been pronounced impossible, as the division of the country into several banking

President Woodrow Wilson

1. The Board of Governors of the Federal Reserve System was known as the Federal Reserve Board until it was renamed by the Banking Act of 1935. The Act strengthened the Board's powers and removed the Secretary of the Treasury and the Comptroller of the Currency from the Board's membership.

districts in each of which there should be a separate and independent institution," Henry Parker Willis wrote in his 1923 book "The Federal Reserve System, a History of the Creation of the Federal Reserve." "On no point had there been sharper controversy than as to the issue whether Banks should be four, eight, 12 or some other number. Yet this politically contested issue, and the much more difficult problem of how to construct the several banking districts, were now to be quickly disposed of by a Committee which had scant time for theoretical inquiry or practical observation."

With lawmakers having various ideas about how to structure the nation's central bank, President Woodrow Wilson's leadership and ability for crafting political compromise were crucial in obtaining legislative approval of the Federal Reserve Act.

ROBERT LATHAM OWEN

Robert L. Owen served Oklahomans in the U.S. Senate from 1907 until 1925. He was one of the state's first two senators.

Among the key figures in the creation of the Federal Reserve was a senator from one of the seven states that later became part of the Tenth Federal Reserve District.

Oklahoma Sen. Robert L. Owen was Senate sponsor of the Federal Reserve Act, co-sponsoring the bill with Virginia Congressman Carter Glass. Together, the two steered the legislation to final approval and President Woodrow Wilson's signature in December 1913.

From East to West

Although Owen made his career in Oklahoma, he was born in Lynchburg, Va., on Feb. 2, 1856, to Robert Owen, president of the Virginia and Tennessee Railway, and Narcissa Clark Chisholm, a woman of Native American, Scottish and English ancestry. Reflecting her own heritage, Narcissa gave her newborn son two names. In addition to Robert, the child was also given the Cherokee name Oconostota - the same name as her great-great-grandfather, who was the tribe's principal chief during the Revolutionary War.

Owen was also related to another important historical figure from the same time period. One of his grandmothers was a grandniece of George Washington - a connection that clearly meant much to Owen, who, as an adult, regularly carried a locket containing a clipping of the first president's hair. It was one of several Washington relics that he owned.

As a 10-year-old, Owen attended school near Baltimore and later graduated from Lexington's Washington and Lee University with honors and a master's degree in 1877.

While Owen was away, his father - after losing his railroad job in a restructuring and starting a brief political career that included an election to the state senate - died abruptly for unknown reasons. The family's fortune was lost to unexplained circumstances, likely related to the Civil War and Reconstruction. The loss forced Owen and his mother to move to the Indian Territory, where they were entitled to tribal property.

While living in what later became Oklahoma, Owen briefly taught school at the Cherokee Orphan Asylum before studying law and gaining admittance to the Bar in 1880. In 1885, he was appointed head of the United States Union Agency for the Five Civilized Tribes.

Owen handled a series of cases involving a number of tribes. Among his more notable victories was a $4 million U.S. Supreme Court ruling against the U.S. government related to the Cherokee's forced removal to

Indian Territory, an event that became known as the Trail of Tears. Owen spent seven years on the case.

Owen also fought against some of the politics that he saw within the Cherokee Nation.

"These activities also won for him a reputation for integrity which later on was of incalculable value in his political career," historian Wyatt W. Belcher wrote in a paper published in the winter 1953 edition of The Chronicles of Oklahoma.

Owen also was involved in real estate and he owned and edited a newspaper in Vinita, Okla. He got into banking in 1890 by establishing the First National Bank of Muskogee, where he served as president until 1900. Owen wrote about his banking experience, and how that related to his later legislative efforts, in his 1919 book, "The Federal Reserve Act: Its Origin and Principles, A Reminiscence."

"In 1890 I had established the First National Bank of Muskogee and in 1893 witnessed the panic that took place at that time," Owen wrote. "This bank, like many other banks, lost 50 percent of its deposits within as many days because of the panic, which frightened people and caused them to withdraw their funds for hoarding throughout the United States."

The panic, Owen wrote, "demonstrated the complete instability of the financial system of America and the hazards which businessmen had to meet under a grossly defective banking system."

In 1896, Owen started working within his political party on banking reform measures designed to prevent panics like the one he had witnessed.

The Senate

When Oklahoma was granted statehood in 1907, voters did not yet have the ability to directly elect senators. Oklahoma residents, however, were given the opportunity to vote in what was known as a preferential primary. Owen was the top vote-getter in a field of seven and, as a result, was appointed to the post by the Oklahoma legislature. With the selection, Owen was not only one of the state's first two senators, but also one of the nation's first two senators of Native American descent, joining Kansan Charles Curtis, a former congressman who also became a senator in 1907.

Owen, who The Los Angeles Times described as "a young man of striking oratorical gifts and great popularity," had many notable Senate accomplishments including the creation of the Senate Banking Committee, for which he served as its first chairman. He was a leader in the direct election of senators and the Child Labor Act, among other issues.

The highlight of Owen's Senate career, however, arguably was his involvement with the Federal Reserve Act.

In his 1919 book, Owen offered insight on the process of creating the Act, which, he wrote, was subject to more than 800 amendments, many related to "language and punctuation, the changing of words back and forth, and matters of that character, which were unimportant."

The history of the legislation dated back to the banking crisis of 1907, which prompted Congress to establish the National Monetary Commission.

Continued on next page

Sen. Owen's book about the Federal Reserve was one of many he authored that was advertised and sold nationwide.

The Federal Reserve Act's approval came after numerous disputes and hours of testimony on both sides of the issue.

After he signed the bill, President Wilson praised Owen's work in a letter to the Oklahoma senator.

"Now that the fight has come to a successful issue, may I not extend to you my most sincere and heartfelt congratulations and also tell you how sincerely I admire the way in which you have conducted a very difficult and trying piece of business?" the president wrote. "The whole country owes you a debt of gratitude and admiration. It has been a pleasure to be associated with you in so great a piece of constructive legislation."

Treasury Secretary William G. McAdoo wrote that Owen's handling of the legislation displayed "qualities of leadership and statemenship which will forever link (Owen) with this immortal measure and give (him) a permanent place in the history of our country."

In 1931, Owen presented the state of Oklahoma with a copy of the Act that he received from Wilson during the 1913 signing ceremony. In correspondence to then-Gov. William H. Murray, Owen called the document, which was printed on vellum, "the most valued relic" of his political life.

Father of the Federal Reserve

While establishing the Federal Reserve may have been Owen's greatest accomplishment, Belcher and other historians have said it was also the cause of Owen's greatest disappointment because most of the credit went to co-sponsor Carter Glass. Glass, who had a far longer political career that included a later stint as Treasury secretary and a Senate seat, is sometimes referred to as the "father of the Federal Reserve."

In later years, "Glass and Owen squabbled with each other very bitterly" about who was the principal author of the Federal Reserve Act, says Dr. Kenny L. Brown, chair of the Department of History and Geography at the University of Central Oklahoma and a leading expert on Owen.

Sen. Owen, second from right, was chair of the Senate Committee on Banking and Currency during the 63rd Congress when the Federal Reserve Act was drafted and approved. Photographed attending this undated Committee meeting with two House counterparts were, from left, Sen. James A. O'Gorman, New York; Rep. Charles A. Korbly, Indiana; Sen. James A. Reed, Missouri; Sen. Henry F. Hollis, New Hampshire; Sen. Atlee Pomerene, Ohio; Sen. Owen; and Sen. John F. Shafroth, Colorado. Writing on the back of the photo indicates Rep. Carter Glass of Virginia was also in attendance at the meeting, but is hidden from view by O'Gorman.

Glass became especially outraged by Owen's 1919 book about Owen's experiences in banking and crafting the Federal Reserve Act.

Owen, meanwhile, likely was angered by a ceremony held to mark the 25th anniversary of the Federal Reserve that focused almost exclusively on Glass. The Dec. 23, 1938 event at the Federal Reserve Board of Governors building in Washington, D.C., included the unveiling of a bronze bas-relief of Glass, with his likeness appearing under the words "Defender of the Federal Reserve System." The relief was placed on a wall opposite a similar portrait of President Wilson.

The unveiling moved Glass to tears, leaving him nearly speechless as he told those in attendance that "my heart is too full for words."

Accounts of the event in the nation's major daily newspapers made no mention of Owen's role in establishing the central bank. However, a few days later, a syndicated columnist named Ray Tucker mentioned the dedication and the ongoing feud between the two men in his column.

According to Tucker, Owen was invited to attend the event, but "when Owen learned that Glass was to be given credit for framing and passing the law, he returned his invitation and expressed regret that he could not attend."

Tucker's column suggests that then-Federal Reserve Chairman Marriner Eccles, who was hoping to win the support of then-Senator Glass, had determined Glass to be the true father of the Federal Reserve.

Brown, the Oklahoma historian, says that determining who was most responsible for the Act is difficult.

"Glass probably is more responsible, but not a whole lot more," Brown says.

According to Brown, Owen and Glass finally resolved their differences after Owen penned a letter to Glass saying that it was time for the dispute to end and noting that both men were raised only a few blocks apart in the same childhood hometown of Lynchburg, Va. Today, both men are buried in Lynchburg's Spring Hill Cemetery.

Later, Owen was also recognized by the Federal Reserve. An area near one of the Federal Reserve buildings in Washington, D.C., is known as Robert Latham Owen Park.

Carter Glass

After retiring from the Senate in 1925, Owen practiced law in Washington, D.C. His primary interest, however, was in promoting the idea of an international alphabet based on phonetics that he hoped would make English a universal language. He spent $25,000 of his own money in developing an alphabet utilizing 41 symbols that the then-blind Owen described to an assistant who drew them.

"It is a means by which we can teach the English language to all the world at high speed and negligible cost," Owen told an Associated Press reporter for a July 1943 article. "It will pay its own way."

Owen told the reporter that the effort was inspired by the Cherokee Chief Sequoia, who developed an 85-character alphabet in 1823 that enabled his tribesmen to learn to write their own language within a few weeks.

Although unsuccessful, Owen's effort generated a significant amount of media attention.

After the death of his wife, Daisy Hester, in 1946, Owen lived the final months of his life alone as a near-invalid in an apartment near Washington's Meridian Hill Park. After being hospitalized for several weeks with an illness and undergoing an operation, he died on July 19, 1947. He was 91.

Twelve Districts

Although the number of Reserve Districts was hotly debated prior to the Act's approval, the issue would be among the first, and perhaps the easiest, for the Committee to resolve.

"There was a Vast amount of state and city pride revealed to us in the hearings…"

It "became obvious that if we created fewer banks than the maximum fixed by law, the Reserve Board would have no peace till that number was reached," Houston wrote. Ballots were sent to 7,741 national banks that had formally assented to the provisions of the Federal Reserve Act asking each their preferences for Reserve Bank cities. The vote, however, was only one component in determining the Reserve Bank locations and the Federal Reserve Districts.

The Committee appointed a Preliminary Committee on Organization, headed by Willis, to address several issues related to the organization of the Federal Reserve, including the drawing of some preliminary District maps.

Meanwhile, the Committee embarked on a tour of the United States under a travel schedule that was aggressive even by modern standards. During a five-week span, Houston and McAdoo would log 10,000 miles, convene hearings in 18 communities and hear presentations from 37 cities. At the end of the tour, they held 5,000 pages of testimony.

The Committee hoped the meetings would be tightly focused on banking and business relationships throughout the country. In announcing the hearing schedule, the Committee said it sought information related only to three key points:

- Geographical convenience, including both transportation and communication.
- Industrial and commercial development, including a consideration of the movement of commodities and business transactions.
- The established custom and trend of business under the existing system of bank reserves.

"Purely local sentiment and pride must yield to the common good in order that the system itself may accomplish the purposes for which it was designed, namely to secure to the business of the country the elastic system of credits and the stability of conditions so long imperatively demanded," the Committee wrote.

The hearings received widespread media attention, fueling public speculation about the Committee's eventual selections and influencing the tone of the discussions. Although the Committee wanted to talk about business and banking relationships, they often found themselves involved in something similar to what is seen today when municipalities court a professional sports franchise or a corporate headquarters.

"There was a vast amount of state and city pride revealed to us in the hearings; and to hear some of the speeches, one would have thought that not to select the city of the advocate would mean its ruin and that of their territory," Houston later wrote.

Regional rivalries were evident in many parts of the country, including within the area that would later become the Tenth Federal Reserve District.

David Franklin Houston,
U.S. Secretary of Agriculture, 1913-20.

William Gibbs McAdoo,
U.S. Treasury Secretary, 1913-18.

RIDING THE RAILS

Before the opening of Union Station, trains arriving in Kansas City, like the one carrying Treasury Secretary William McAdoo and Agriculture Secretary David Houston, came to the Union Depot in the city's West Bottoms. The flood-prone station, built in 1869, was too small to serve the growing city and was replaced when Union Station opened on Oct. 30, 1914.

Although the prospect of a lengthy cross-country tour and a series of hearings was likely a daunting proposition for the Reserve Bank Organizing Committee, the members decided almost immediately that the trip was a necessity.

Charged with determining the flow of the nation's business, Treasury Secretary William G. McAdoo and Agriculture Secretary David F. Houston realized the tour offered many benefits.

From a logistical standpoint, the tour would be far simpler than inviting hundreds of the country's business and banking leaders to attend sessions in Washington, D.C. The tour could also be quickly scheduled – the Committee announced plans for its tour after its first formal meeting on Dec. 26 and hoped to hold its first public hearing a week later on Jan. 2, 1914. That hearing, however, was delayed into the following week when McAdoo became ill.

For the journey west, starting with a hearing Jan. 19 in Chicago, the Committee acquired a railcar that numerous media accounts described as "a steel car of the latest type." It was called "National."

According to a story in the Jan. 2, 1914 *Washington Post*, the railcar was cheaper than booking traditional rail passage. *The Post* reporter also noted that, for a Committee that was very much in the national spotlight, the railcar provided an office "where they can retire and avoid persistent boosters urging the claims of their cities for Reserve Banks."

It was an unprecedented trip that some found comparable only to the traveling party of a president.

The Post reporter predicted the tour would employ "a little government army" comprising secretaries; four stenographers; a couple of messengers; and even, perhaps, a Treasury Department attorney. Newspaper accounts from various stops along the journey, however, indicate it was a smaller group. In addition to McAdoo and Houston, in Kansas City the traveling party included:

- George R. Cooksey, McAdoo's secretary;
- Thomas A. Gray, McAdoo's private secretary;
- W.F. Callander, Houston's secretary.

Also on the trip was McAdoo's 16-year-old daughter, Nona, one of six children McAdoo had with his first wife who had died two years earlier. Nona also brought along a friend, Ellen Robinson. Finally, it was not uncommon for a rail line representative to travel with the Committee on some legs of the journey to assist with travel arrangements.

The third member of the Committee, Comptroller of the Currency John Skelton Williams, whose appointment was delayed in the U.S. Senate, joined the group at a Feb. 13 stop in Atlanta and participated in the final two stops in Cincinnati and Cleveland. After being unable to take part in earlier tour stops, Williams had planned to meet the Committee when it returned to Washington at the trip's conclusion. A story in the Feb. 12, 1914 edition of *The Washington Post* said Williams changed his mind about the tour because "the situation in Ohio ... is expected to prove rather delicate," suggesting Committee members expected problems in Ohio with multiple cities seeking a Bank.

Back East

After concluding the tour, the Committee issued a lengthy statement that revealed nothing about possible Reserve Bank Districts or cities, but talked about the widespread support the Committee found for the nation's new central bank.

The statement also offered some insight on several areas of interest, including:

- What they learned about the national economy:

"Facts and figures submitted to the committee in every part of the country show amazing growth and strength, and disclosed a condition of financial, industrial, commercial and agricultural soundness and prosperity that leaves no doubt as to the future."

- What the Committee saw as its most significant challenge:

"We have spent practically from the fourth of January to the present time in hearing the views of businessmen and bankers on the problem of dividing the country into not less than eight nor more than 12 Districts and of locating in each District the main office of a Federal Reserve Bank. Of the two questions, the division of the country into Districts is the more important and difficult."

- How the Committee expected the process to move forward:

"The committee has finished its survey in the field. It has yet to make examination of important documents and data, and cannot render any decision until it has thoroughly examined this material. It can come to no conclusion about any part of the country until it has formed its conclusions for every part of the country, since the Districts are necessarily interrelated and interdependent. It cannot, of course, decide the location of headquarters Banks until the Districts are defined."

EN ROUTE
PULLMAN PRIVATE CAR *National*

at Lincoln, Neb. 7 am!
Jany 24 —

Emil I had the right to begin
this letter with the most beau-
tiful word in the English
language — Sweetheart —
but as you haven't given
it to me, I can't — So I
must begin with something
that does not imply pos-
session (Alas!) but is
merely descriptive and
expressive of my own
feelings. Sweet angel,
you are so perfect, and
yet you have disclosed

A day after leaving Kansas City, William McAdoo wrote a letter to his fiancée, Eleanor Wilson, while his train was in Lincoln, Neb. In the letter, only a portion of which remains, McAdoo mentions receiving a telegram from Wilson during his Kansas City stop. As McAdoo toured the nation, Wilson was preparing for the couple's wedding, which was held May 7, 1914, in the White House.

A.W. Field, who was one of the two lead speakers in favor of locating a Reserve Bank in Lincoln, Neb., said that he and fellow presenter P.L. Hall agreed prior to their remarks that, if the Committee asked, both would voice support for Omaha as their second choice.

The Committee did not ask, but Field, who listened to Omaha's presentation before he made Lincoln's pitch, later told *The Lincoln Daily Star* that he may not have kept the agreement.

"I don't know that I would have said it … after I got up there and witnessed the attitude of the Omaha men," Field said in the newspaper's April 3, 1914 edition. "All reference to Lincoln was made with an open sneer and I didn't like it. I am not usually a man who will turn the other cheek when I have been slapped and I interpreted Omaha's attitude as a slap. There is no other conclusion. Omaha's attitude hurt Lincoln's chance to be considered and I think Lincoln's failure to join hands with Omaha hurt that city."

The media also criticized the behavior of local civic boosters across the United States.

"The hearings of the Reserve Bank organizers, generally speaking, have been more remarkable for the local jealousies they have disclosed than for the perception that there was anything of national significance in the new departure," *The New York Times* wrote in an editorial.

In an attempt to return an appropriate tone to the hearings, McAdoo said several times publicly that the selection as a Reserve Bank city was not as important to future economic development as some citizens appeared to believe. The issue also was touched upon later in a statement issued by the Committee days after their selections were announced.

"It became clear in the hearings that comparatively few people realized, or seemed to realize, what the Act was intended to accomplish; what the nature and functions of the Reserve Banks were to be;

and how little change would occur in the ordinary financial relations of the communities, the business establishments and the individual banks," the Committee wrote.

In his book, Willis, who went on to become the first secretary to the Federal Reserve Board, says would-be Federal Reserve cities "saw in the new banking system, a means of self-aggrandizing or self-advertising.

"Much of the testimony and many of the briefs that were filed read like land or travel prospectuses in which the good gifts of Providence to the different parts of the country were enumerated in the most glowing colors. The political aspects of the game soon took precedence of other considerations and the question became fundamental how to satisfy the greatest possible number of the places which were demanding the assignment of a Bank."

> "The *Political Aspects* of the game soon took precedence of other considerations and the question became fundamental how to satisfy the greatest possible number of the places…"

The Committee also was forced to regularly refute the belief held by many that politics would play an important role in the location of the regional Banks.

During the Chicago hearing, a banker presenting St. Paul, Minn.'s bid for a regional Bank received a quick and angry response from both McAdoo and Houston after telling the Committee that his community was "a great Democratic city, if that has any bearing."

"It has not," McAdoo responded. "That is the last fact that would have any bearing. This is an economic question, not a political one."

McAdoo mentioned the exchange in a Jan. 24, 1914 letter to his fiancée, Eleanor Wilson, daughter of the president. In it, McAdoo describes the St. Paul speaker as a flustered, "red faced man who floundered terribly.

"The St. Paul delegation was tremendously disturbed by his break and I am somewhat fearful for the poor man's life if we decide (as we probably shall) against St. Paul."

A Case *for* Kansas City

In Kansas City, the effort to win a regional Reserve Bank started with Jerome Thralls.

Even while lawmakers were still crafting the bill, the manager of the Kansas City Clearing House Association started working to convince bankers that Kansas City should pursue one of the new regional Reserve Banks. An article in the Dec. 23, 1913 edition of *The Kansas City Times* about final work on the Federal Reserve Act in Washington is accompanied by a brief story noting that local bankers had met at the Kansas City Clearing House Association's offices the previous day to start on a plan to win one of the Banks for Kansas City.

"The bankers at the meeting – and every bank in the Clearing House Association was represented – were unanimous in the belief that Kansas City, by all means, must obtain one of the Reserve Banks," Thralls told a reporter. "We feel that the importance of Kansas City as the center of a great trading district demands it."

Thralls accomplished much in getting the bankers to support his vision. Although *The Kansas City Times* later wrote that the city's campaign for the Bank "was one of the most determined in its history," Thralls initially found little support for his idea.

"At first most (Kansas City bankers) thought it was a forlorn hope," *The Kansas City Journal* wrote later after Kansas City's selection was announced. "Thralls was confident and he believed differently. He insisted that there was a territory belonging to Kansas City which would supply such a Bank with all needed capital and surplus."

The Kansas City Times wrote about Thralls' initial meeting with an unidentified president of one of the city's largest banks who reportedly told Thralls: "I admire your courage, but I am afraid it would be a useless task."

It would not be the only time Thralls would find resistance to the idea.

"Other bankers were inclined to think he was too ambitious, but he said he was willing to do the work if they would get behind him," *The Times* reported.

Eventually, bankers warmed to Thralls' idea and the communitywide effort began to take shape.

Thralls and other members of the Kansas City Clearing House Association then began working to convince Missouri's representatives in Washington that Kansas City was a worthy location.

Kansas City, a booming regional hub, made a strong case for why it should be selected as home to one of the regional Reserve Banks. This photo from 1915 shows the city much as it was when Kansas Citians were readying their case to win one of the Banks. The street on the left side of the photo is Grand Avenue heading north toward downtown.

Jerome Thralls

FIRST SECRETARY *and* CASHIER

Jerome Thralls' image was on the front page of The Kansas City Journal *on April 3, 1914, when the paper reported that Kansas City had been selected as a site for one of the Federal Reserve Banks.*

Although his tenure as the first secretary and cashier of the Federal Reserve Bank of Kansas City was brief, few individuals played a more pivotal role in its history than Jerome Thralls.

The campaign to win over the Reserve Bank Organizing Committee involved many of the city's business leaders, but it was Thralls who first presented the idea to local bankers. He convinced the community it could win one of the Regional Banks, and he did much of the work in preparing the city's presentation.

Then, a little more than a year after the Bank opened, Thralls left Kansas City, taking a job on the East Coast. He became an authority on international trade with an office in the middle of New York's financial district - a long way from his humble beginnings in rural Missouri.

Early years

The youngest of Henry and Margaret Thralls' nine children, Jerome Thralls grew up in the small town of Chillicothe. His first job in an eclectic string of positions paid him 50 cents a day to pitch hay for a neighbor.

According to a 1926 *Kansas City Star* article, after pitching hay, Thralls worked building chicken coops before taking a job in a rural general merchandise store. He was later involved in small town real estate and banking, and he earned $800 for six months as a fur trapper in the Ozarks.

He spent five years with an express company, a job he sought after reading a newspaper article that mentioned the hefty salary paid to the company's president.

"I decided that I should like nothing better than to be president of that great company and I headed at once for the job," Thralls said in *The Star* article.

Clearing House Manager Who Initiated Move For Federal Reserve Bank Here

JEROME THRALLS.

KANSAS CITY IS CHOSEN AS SITE OF RESERVE BANK

District With Capital of $5,594,916 Comprises Four States and Parts of Two Others.

TWELVE INSTITUTIONS ARE LOCATED IN U. S.

Nation Is Divided Into Sections Which Vary Little in Population, With a Pair of Exceptions.

DISAPPOINTED TOWNS MAY ENTER PROTEST

Keen Rivalry Was Feature of Contest for Selection; Decision Is Not Likely to Be Revised.

Reserve Bank Cities	
KANSAS CITY.	ATLANTA.
NEW YORK.	CHICAGO.
PHILADELPHIA.	ST. LOUIS.
BOSTON.	MINNEAPOLIS.
CLEVELAND.	DALLAS.
RICHMOND.	SAN FRANCISCO.

He did not make it to company president, but the job took him to Kansas City, where he was later offered a position with the Kansas City Clearing House Association, an organization involved in routing payments between banks. When lawmakers approved the Federal Reserve Act in December 1913, Thralls was the Association's manager - a position that gave him unique insight on the relationships of the region's banks. The 32-year-old

Pointe Cour
Terre Bonne.

District No. ... Chicago. Capital $16,-
151,925, with 984 national banks and a
number of state banks and trust companies. Territory—Iowa, Wisconsin,
south of the northern boundary of the
following counties: Vernon, Sauk,
Columbia, Dodge, Washington and
Osaukee; all of the southern peninsula
of Michigan; Illinois north of a line
forming the southern boundary of the
following counties: Hancock, Schuyler,
Cass, Sangamon, Christian, Shelby,
Cumberland and Clark; Indiana north of
a line forming the southern boundary of
the following counties: Vigo, Clay, Owen,
Monroe, Brown, Bartholomew, Jennings,
Ripley and Ohio.

Missouri Is Divided.

District No. 8, St. Louis. Capital
$6,219,313, with 434 national banks and a
number of state banks and trust companies. Territory—Arkansas, Missouri,
east of the western boundary of the following counties: Harrison, Daviess,
Caldwell, Ray, Lafayette, Johnson,
Henry, St. Clair, Cedar, Dade, Lawrence
and Barry; Illinois not included in District 7; Indiana not in District 7; Kentucky not in District 4; Tennessee not
in District 6, and Mississippi not in District 8.

District No. 9, Minneapolis. Capital
$4,702,864, with 687 national banks and a
number of state banks and trust companies. Territory—Montana, North Dakota, South Dakota, Minnesota, Wisconsin and Michigan not in District
No. 7.

District No. 10, Kansas City, Capital
$5,594,416, with 885 national banks and sev-
eral state banks and trust companies.
Territory—Kansas, Nebraska, Colorado,
Wyoming, Missouri not in District No. 8,
Oklahoma north of a line forming the
southern boundary of the following
counties: Ellis, Dewey, Blaine, Canad-
ian, Cleveland, Pottawatomie, Sem-
inole, Okfuskee, McIntosh, Muskogee and
Sequoyah; New Mexico north of a line
forming the southern boundary of the
following counties: McKinley, Sandova,
Santa Fe, San Miguel and Union.

District No. 11, Dallas. Capital $5,634,091,
with 726 national banks and several state
banks and trust companies. Territory—
Texas, New Mexico and Oklahoma not
in District No. 10; Louisiana not in District 6 and the following counties in
Arizona: Pima, Graham, Greenlee,
Cochise and Santa Cruz.

District No. 12, San Francisco. Capital
$8,115,514, with 514 national banks and sev-
eral state banks and trust companies.
Territory—California, Washington, Oregon, Idaho, Nevada and Utah, and Arizona not included in District No. 11.

Branch Banks Later.

The organization committee was not authorized by law to provide for branch
banks of the federal reserve banks, but
the act specifically states that such banks
shall be established. This task will be
left to the supervision of the federal reserve board, yet to be appointed by President Wilson. The organization committee announced that all information it has
collected since it began its work last

No. 10, area in square miles, 509,649;
population, 6,306,850.
No. 11, area in square miles, 404,826;
population, 5,310,551.
No. 12, area in square miles, 693,658;
population, 5,309,393.

According to this statement there will
be at least 7,548 banks of all sorts members of the system, with a total capital
and surplus of $1,631,648,369. Their 6 per
cent subscriptions would amount to $109,-
898,902, according to the committee's
figures.

Three Months' Secret Work.

The organization committee, Secretaries
McAdoo, Houston and Comptroller of the
Currency Williams, have spent most of
their time for the last three months on
this work. Extraordinary precautions
prevented knowledge from reaching out-
siders, and even members of congress
were denied information until the announcement was made.

Although the progress of organizing the
new system will not be rapid, it is the
intention of the committee to act as
quickly as the law permits in order that
the reserve banks may be set up for
business as soon as possible.

The usual statement of the comptroller
following the last national bank call issued showed the banks in excellent condition to meet the demands shortly to be
made for subscriptions to reserve bank
stock. It is the hope of the committee
that the gradual transitions necessary under the new law will be made easily,
without disturbance and without any cur-
tailment of credit.

The rivalry between many cities for
reserve banks was intense and the committee's decision may be followed by pro-
tests and attempts to change the plan.
Under the law the decision is not subject to revision, except by the federal reserve board, and it was believed tonight
that the board will consider a long time
before it will attempt to make any
changes.

Some of the cities in the race for banks
which were not selected were Baltimore,
Washington, Birmingham, Ala.; New Or-
leans, Cincinnati, Louisville, Omaha, St.
Paul, Denver, Houston, Tex.; Seattle,
Portland, Oregon and Los Angeles.

MOST CREDIT DUE THRALLS

**Clearing House Manager Started
K. C. After Bank and Kept at It.**

There were no happier men in Greater
Kansas City last night than the bankers,
who have been on the anxious seat for
weeks awaiting the report of the federal
bank organization committee from Washington. The fact that Kansas City is to
get one of the great government banks
is due to the efforts of the bankers of
Greater Kansas City and bankers in the
district which originally was claimed by
this city.

Members of the Kansas City Clearing

Continued on Page 2, Column 5.

*Although Thralls' name is unknown to modern-day Kansas Citians, newspaper
headlines in 1914 said that he was the reason the city would host one of the 12
regional Reserve Banks.*

immediately started contacting local bankers to discuss a possible Federal
Reserve Bank in Kansas City.

"It was Mr. Thralls who ... called a meeting of the local bankers and
urged them at once to go after one of the Banks," *The Kansas City Journal*
later wrote. The bankers were unsure about the city's chances, but Thralls
eventually won them over, beginning what would become a communitywide effort.

The best-case scenario

His efforts resulted in a Kansas City visit by the Reserve
Bank Organizing Committee where Thralls presented
each panel member with a leather-bound report detailing
why Kansas City was an ideal location for one of the
regional Banks. Although the committee received similar
filings from 36 other communities nationwide, the Kansas
City report "was more concise, contained more real meat
and was in better shape than any which had been
filed with the committee," *The Kansas City Journal*
later reported.

The front page of the newspaper's April 3, 1914 edition,
which announced Kansas City's selection, featured a hand-
drawn portrait of Thralls next to the headline announcing the
news. Another front page headline proclaimed: "Most Credit
Due Thralls. Clearing House Manager Started K.C. After
Bank and Kept At It."

Thralls was described as "modest and unassuming"
in the 1926 *Star* story. The assessment seems accurate
based on his brief public comments in what must have
been among the proudest moments of his life. Asked by
a reporter about his feelings upon learning the city's
selection, Thralls said he was "highly gratified."

He showed only a little more emotion a day later at a
boisterous gathering of the local business leaders celebrating the city's
selection. At an event featuring at least one vaudeville-style performer,
music and three hours of speeches eliciting laughter and applause, Thralls'
brief comments were a stoic departure from the other speakers.

"We came nearer getting the territory we asked for than any other
city," Thralls said. "That shows we were honest and sincere in presenting
our case. We asked only for what rightfully belonged to us. I have been here
12 years and it's the greatest of Kansas City's victories in that time."

Continued on next page

The Federal Reserve and beyond

The Federal Reserve Bank of Kansas City's Board of Directors chose Thralls to serve as the Bank's first cashier and secretary during its meeting on Oct. 31, 1914, about two weeks before it opened for business.

"I shall support Mr. Thralls for cashier, and that for the reason that nearly every bank in town is supporting him for that position and expects him to have it," Director and future Bank Gov. Willis J. Bailey told the Bank's other directors during the meeting.

Thralls' stay at the Bank, however, was relatively brief. He resigned Feb. 10, 1916, to accept a position with the American Bankers Association. According to Bank records, Thralls' resignation was accepted and "a most complimentary resolution of regret and appreciation" was adopted by the Board of Directors.

Likely because of his popularity with local bankers, and his role in winning the Bank's headquarters, Thralls' departure produced a minor controversy.

A newspaper article published by *The Kansas City Journal* two weeks before Thralls' departure suggested he was being forced out as politicians attempted to politicize the nation's new central bank. Thralls was a Republican and the article suggested there was pressure from Washington to place Democrats in the top positions at each of the regional Reserve Banks. The article suggested that the pressure may have even prevented Thralls from an initial appointment to the Bank's top position.

"The bankers of Kansas City recognized the ability of Mr. Thralls and after Kansas City had been selected as the location of one of the Federal Reserve Banks, he had many endorsements to head the institution as Federal Reserve agent and chairman of the Board of Directors," the article says. "His political affiliation is believed to have kept him out of that."

Jerome Thralls

Thralls, who was out of town interviewing for the ABA position when the story was published, sent a letter to the newspaper refuting the article's claims and voicing his support for both the Bank and the entire Federal Reserve System.

"My connection with the Federal Reserve Bank ... has no relation whatever to politics and when I leave the service of the Federal Reserve Bank of Kansas City it will be for the purpose of engaging in a line of work which will afford a broader field of activity, and with matters of common interest to the members of the Federal Reserve System," Thralls wrote in the letter dated Feb. 2, 1916.

After leaving the Bank, Thralls went on to great success.

At the ABA, he was once again involved with clearinghouses and he served in an advisory capacity to the government's financing program for World War I. He authored a textbook, became a recognized expert on foreign trade and was involved in the formation of the American Trade Acceptance Council. He served as vice president of the Discount Corporation of New York and, later in his career, became president of the Prudence Securities Corporation.

He died on March 19, 1965, at the age of 84 in Brooklyn, N.Y.

In *The Star's* 1926 article, Thralls was asked about the various career opportunities he had pursued, with the reporter suggesting that chance is a key component of life.

"I wouldn't call it chance," Thralls said. "I'd call it opportunity. We are, in a measure, creatures of environment and opportunity. Some see and grasp every opportunity for advancement in life, while others let the opportunity slip by. It was opportunity to work in the neighbor's hay field that gave me my first half dollar and the inspiration to earn more."

James Reed

A telegram seeking support was sent to Congressman William P. Borland. The group also sought meetings with the state's two senators. Although Sen. William J. Stone, a St. Louis resident, was unable to meet, the group spent a Sunday afternoon with the state's junior senator, Kansas City's James A. Reed. He was won over and returned to Washington to take up the fight.

Still, when the Reserve Bank Organizing Committee announced its travel itinerary, Kansas City was not on the list. After spending three days in St. Louis, the Committee planned to head west to Denver for a one-day session. In announcing its travel schedule, the Committee said it would not consider any additions to the list.

But the Committee finally agreed to extend what Worley called a "courtesy" to Kansas City. Likely because of the work of Missouri's Congressional delegation, the Committee agreed to spend part of a Friday – a day slated for St. Louis under the original schedule – listening to a presentation in one of the Kansas City's federal courtrooms.

In preparation for the meeting, groups of Kansas City bankers traveled throughout the region to build support, visiting cities including Denver, Omaha, Oklahoma City, Albuquerque and even Dallas.

Missouri Sen. James A. Reed did much work in Washington, D.C., to assist with the bid to win a regional Reserve Bank. Before serving in the Senate, Reed was Kansas City's mayor from 1900 to 1904 and oversaw one of the most historic events in Kansas City history: the construction of a new convention hall in 1900. The hall was built in only 90 days—in time to host the Democratic National Convention, which had been slated for a previous facility that was destroyed by fire three months earlier.

River, rail *and* the renowned stockyards

With the Missouri River nearby and a nearly non-stop rumble of trains along the city's railroad tracks, Kansas City in 1913 found itself in the enviable position of serving as a national crossroads. It was a location ideal for business, industry – and, as Kansas Citians believed, a Federal Reserve Bank.

The city was home to the two largest mail-order houses west of the Mississippi operated by Montgomery Ward & Co. and Sears, Roebuck & Co. Manufacturing was a major employer with some 40,000 residents of the greater Kansas City area employed by the region's 1,200 factories. Kansas City led the nation in farm equipment sales and was a major player in the lumber market, leading the nation in the sale of yellow pine.

But for all its industry and manufacturing, Kansas City's heart was the stockyards.

Although the famous stockyards were an important part of Kansas City, the local economy also featured numerous manufacturers and retailers—businesses that could take advantage of the city's role as the major river and rail hub for a large portion of the central and southwestern United States.

At the turn of the century, the famed Kansas City stockyards covered more than 50 acres and were the second busiest in the nation, trailing only Chicago. More than 2.3 million cattle, 3 million hogs and 2 million sheep made their way through Kansas City in 1913. The city was also a major player in the poultry and egg business as well as in the horse and mule markets.

It is probably no coincidence that the city's population enjoyed a boom that can be traced back to the yards' establishment in the late 1800s.

According to U.S. Census data, the city's population grew more than 50 percent between 1900 and 1910 to nearly 250,000 residents. The growth continued in the 1910s as the city swelled to nearly 325,000 residents in 1920 – up 30 percent from a decade earlier.

MISSOURI RIVER SCENE.

If the stockyards were the city's heart, however, the railroads were its lifeline. In addition to the livestock industry, local wholesalers and manufacturers were able to ship their products on some of the 2,000 freight cars that rolled in and out of the city every day thanks to the Atchison, Topeka and Santa Fe; Kansas City Southern; Union Pacific; and 13 other trunk rail lines that served the city, in addition to 32 subordinate lines.

To better handle the amount of rail traffic passing through the growing community, the city was nearing completion on the construction of Union Station. The massive facility would replace a flood-damaged Union Depot in the city's West Bottoms that was overrun with traffic and handled more pieces of baggage annually than any other station in the world. The new Union Station would be the nation's third-largest train station when it opened, with terminals easily capable of serving the 260 passenger trains that came into and left the city every day.

The mere size of the new train station says much about Kansas City's optimism in the early 1900s. In his 1992 book, "Kansas City, Missouri, An Architectural History, 1826-1990," George Ehrlich writes that the station was "built for a metropolis of a million or more residents" – nearly four times the city's population at the time.

The Committee Hearing

McAdoo and Houston, the two members of the Reserve Bank Organizing Committee who made the Kansas City stop, arrived by train from St. Louis at 9:30 on the morning of Jan. 23.

Before the hearing, a Kansas City reporter asked McAdoo about the city's chances.

"I don't care to talk for publication about the Bank location problem," McAdoo responded. "I'm merely a sponge absorbing all the information I can. I will talk about Kansas City and the Reserve Banks when the time comes."

The men refused an offer of a ride around the city, noting that their train was 30 minutes late and that they were eager to begin the hearing.

On the way to the session it is likely the pair saw the morning's *Kansas City Times*. At least the newspaper's editors apparently hoped the Committee would receive a copy. Much of the paper's front

Although it was officially a three-member committee, a delay in the appointment of John Skelton Williams as Comptroller of the Currency left William McAdoo and David Houston as a two-man panel for most of the Reserve Bank Organizing Committee hearings.

Associated Banks
of Greater Kansas City

As a part of the effort to convince the Reserve Bank Organizing Committee to locate a Federal Reserve Bank in Kansas City, The Associated Banks of Greater Kansas City printed a pamphlet including maps, charts and numerous statistics related to banking and business. The pamphlet was prefaced with this letter:

Kansas City, Mo. Jan. 23, 1914

To the Reserve Bank Organization Committee:

Gentlemen: We believe it is the purpose of your honorable body, as well as the intent of the Federal Reserve Act, that the Federal Reserve Banks provided for under said Act shall be established at points where they will best serve the contiguous territory.

Kansas City, with her splendid railroad facilities and excellent mail service, has become the natural market, financial and distributing center of the richest and most rapidly developing agricultural and mineral district in America.

A large number of the national banks, state banks and trust companies throughout this great territory have signified their intention of becoming members of a Federal Reserve Bank at the earliest possible date, and have expressed their desire to help in every way to make the plan a success. On behalf of these institutions, and the banks and trust companies of Greater Kansas City (Kansas City, Mo., and Kansas City, Kan.), we respectfully submit, for your earnest consideration, the application of this city for the location of one of the Federal Reserve Banks. We believe a Federal Reserve Bank located here could serve more advantageously than if located in any other city; the District including the states of Kansas, Nebraska, New Mexico and Oklahoma, the western part of the state of Missouri, a small part of the states of Arkansas and Iowa, the northern part of the state of Texas and that part of the state of Colorado east of the Rockies. We are submitting herewith data which proves Kansas City's supremacy in this territory and which we hope will enable your honorable body to place its stamp of approval upon this application.

The Federal Reserve Bank of Kansas City, with the District as above outlined, would be a commanding institution, with ample capital and deposits to protect and properly care for the legitimate business needs of this district.

If any further information is desired, we will be glad to furnish it at your command.

Wishing your honorable committee success in the important work of organizing this great system of Federal Reserve Banks, and assuring you of our most hearty support at all times, we are,

Sincerely yours,

The Associated Banks of Greater Kansas City

page was devoted to the day's hearing. At the top of the page, a drawing depicted a figure standing over Kansas City on a map with lines extending across the central United States. Above it was the headline "Here is the Center, There is the Circumference." Front page headlines proclaimed it to be "Kansas City's Day," and promised a Reserve Bank established in Kansas City "Will Be the Best Bank!"

> *"The facts of business have made Kansas City... the inevitable site for one of the Federal Reserve Banks."*

"The facts of business have made Kansas City – not Kansas City, Mo., or Kansas City, Kan., but Kansas City – the inevitable site for one of the Federal Reserve Banks," one article begins.

The Committee was taken by car to the Federal Building downtown on the east side of Grand Avenue between Eighth and Ninth streets – only a block away from where the Bank would later open for business. There, they were welcomed by an overflow crowd of more than 2,000 people spilling down the building's steps and into the street. The crowd continued inside where the Committee was seated at the front of a courtroom filled to capacity with 500 people, mostly bankers.

"The crowd filled the space (in) back of the judge's bench, overflowed into the judge's chambers and into the corridors. The aisles were jammed," *The Kansas City Post* wrote in its Jan. 23, 1914 edition.

McAdoo and Houston sat behind a long table placed in front of the judge's bench. Behind them, a trio of stenographers took turns recording testimony at the court clerk's desk.

The room included a pair of massive wall-size maps. To the Committee's right was one showing the location of each of the region's commercial banks. Nearby was another indicating the region's mail facilities.

The hearing started a half-hour late at 10:30 a.m.

"Bankers, wholesalers, jobbers representing Kansas City and its trade territory took the stand one after the other, and without asking any favors, without oratory and without invoking local pride or sentiment, laid before the Committee the facts upon which Kansas City claimed recognition," *The Kansas City Star* wrote of the Jan. 23 meeting.

The Associated Banks of Greater Kansas City presented a plan for a Federal Reserve District that

The Circulation of THE POST Yesterday Was: CITY, 75,553; TOTAL, 129,101

THE KANSAS CITY POST

O Justice, when expelled from other habitations, make this thy dwelling place.

THE PEOPLE'S NEWSPAPER   KANSAS CITY, MO., FRIDAY, JANUARY 23, 1914.   FOR ALL KINDS OF PEOPLE

BIGGEST CROWD EVER IN K. C. FEDERAL COURT ROOM ASSEMBLES TO HEAR ARGUMENTS FOR FEDERAL BANK

FEDERAL BANK ORGANIZATION BOARD IN SESSION THIS MORNING IN THE KANSAS CITY FEDERAL BUILDING.

wer right is Secretary Houston. At his right is Secretary McAdoo. At right below map—Kansas City business men and bankers. Opposite the two secretaries across the table is President Goebel of the Kansas City Clearing house. Back of him—Interested persons who crowded into the federal court room to attend the hearing.

biggest crowd ever in the federal room listened this morning to guments for the establishing of ral reserve bank in Kansas City. 500 men, principally bankers, l the room. cabinet officers sat back of a

long, wide table in front of the judge's bench. Back of them, at the court clerk's desk, sat three interstate commerce commission stenographers, working in relays. The inclosure for attorneys was crowded with bankers, there as witnesses.

The crowd filled the space back of the judge's bench, overflowed into the judge's chambers and into the corridors. The aisles were jammed. It was difficult to keep such a large crowd quiet and at first little heed was paid to the tapping of Secretary McAdoo's

gavel—a pearl handled knife. After the secretary had explained that absolute quiet was necessary, the quiet voice of Secretary Houston could be heard all over the room.

On the north wall of the room hung a great map of the central western part

of the country, showing Kansas City tributary territory, and a dot for the location of each bank in the district. Another big map on the east wall showed the mail facilities.

At 10 o'clock, when the committee was scheduled to arrive at the federal

building, a crowd of 2,000 people crowded the steps of the building, the sidewalk and part of the street. A larger crowd was waiting when the committee adjourned. A man with a motion picture camera was there to make a record of the doings of the committee.

The Kansas City Post, *Jan. 23, 1914*

included western Missouri; southwest Iowa; all of Nebraska, Kansas, Oklahoma and New Mexico; part of Colorado; the northern half of Texas; and western Arkansas.

"Kansas City, with her splendid railroad facilities and excellent mail service, has become the natural market, financial and distributing center of the richest and most rapidly developing agricultural and mineral district in America," the bankers' group said in written testimony that was presented to the

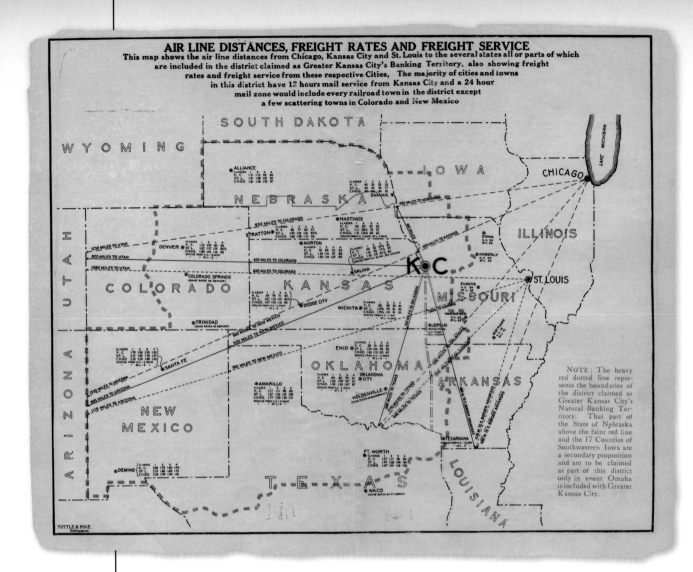

AIR LINE DISTANCES, FREIGHT RATES AND FREIGHT SERVICE

This map shows the air line distances from Chicago, Kansas City and St. Louis to the several states all or parts of which are included in the district claimed as Greater Kansas City's Banking Territory, also showing freight rates and freight service from these respective Cities. The majority of cities and towns in this district have 12 hours mail service from Kansas City and a 24 hour mail zone would include every railroad town in the district except a few scattering towns in Colorado and New Mexico

NOTE: The heavy red dotted line represents the boundaries of the district claimed as Greater Kansas City's Natural Banking Territory. That part of the State of Nebraska above the faint red line and the 17 Counties of Southwestern Iowa are a secondary proposition and are to be claimed as part of this district only in event Omaha is included with Greater Kansas City.

Kansas City's pitch to the Reserve Bank Organizing Committee included charts and maps depicting the city's connection to other parts of the country and its role in the region's business and industry.

Committee in a leather-bound volume on which each Committee member's name was embossed in gold on the cover.

"I must say to you now, Mr. McAdoo and Mr. Houston, that the Bank which you will establish in Kansas City will prove to be one of the most important, useful and successful of the 12 Federal Reserve Banks," F.P. Neal, the Kansas City contingent's chairman and president of Southwest National Bank, told the committee.

Neal was also the committee member who responded when McAdoo asked if Kansas City would be well-served by a branch of another city's Federal Reserve Bank.

The secretary's comment caused a "rastle of dissent all over the audience," *The Star* reported, with Neal rising to tell the committee that "Kansas City didn't want a branch bank because it was not a branch city."

According to *The Star*, McAdoo "smiled broadly and brought his tilted chair back to the table.

"'I ought to say,' he said with extended hand, 'that any question the Committee may ask is not to be interpreted as indicating in any way that the Committee's mind is made up.'"

The local effort to generate support for the Bank headquarters from outside of Kansas City was successful. Of the 30 witnesses testifying before the Committee, all but eight were from outside of the city. Among the strongest of the out-of-state supporters was W.S. Guthrie, president of the Farmers' National Bank of Oklahoma City, who told the Committee that most Oklahoma bankers favored Kansas City.

"Our secretary sent out a letter to every banker in the state. We asked them to express their opinions as to the location of the Reserve Banks. All letters were answered. Eighty percent of them favored Kansas City for the Reserve Bank of Oklahoma," Guthrie said.

The farthest-traveled speaker was P.C. Dings from Ardmore, a south-central Oklahoma community a mere 35 miles from the Texas line. Dings told the Committee that bankers in his city unanimously supported Kansas City.

F.P. Neal, president of Southwest National Bank, chaired the effort to locate a regional Reserve Bank in Kansas City.

He was asked if his city wouldn't be better served by a Bank located in either Forth Worth or Dallas.

"Well, one of them might do as a second choice if we can't have Oklahoma City for our second choice, but Kansas City is our first choice," he responded.

A courtroom inside the Federal Building was the site of the Jan. 23, 1914 Reserve Bank Organizing Committee hearing in Kansas City. The building, which also housed a post office, stood along Grand Avenue between Eighth and Ninth Streets from 1900 until 1938.

Other speakers included Kansas Gov. George Hodges, and his predecessor, Walter Stubbs.

Hodges told the Committee while he personally preferred the Kansas side of the state line, he had no qualms with the regional Reserve Bank being located in Kansas City, Mo.

"Three quarters of the people on the Missouri side are Kansans anyway," Hodges told the Committee.

Stubbs' comments were similar.

"Kansas City is where we want our Bank. If not on the Kansas side, then over here (in Missouri), it makes little difference," Stubbs said. "Kansas brains and Kansas men have made Kansas City. This is a Kansas city and you can't beat it."

The sense of unity between the two Kansas Cities may have surprised a Committee that, throughout the hearing process, regularly heard cities attack one another during their presentations. Only a few days earlier the Committee listened as both Minneapolis and St. Paul sought one of the regional Banks. The Committee also found a similar situation in Texas, where both Dallas and neighboring Fort Worth were among the cities vying for a Bank.

Accounts of the Kansas City event show no comments critical of any community, let alone the one on the other side of the state line. The civil tone of the hearing was noted in the opening lines of

The Kansas City Times' story about the event:

"The hearing … was unique in that the claims of no other city were attacked. The Kansas City witnesses confined themselves to a straightforward statement of the city's business, the extent of its territory and the preferences of businesses in that territory."[2]

Although the Kansas City Clearing House Association had planned to host a dinner for McAdoo and Houston, the cabinet secretaries had to catch their 6:35 p.m. train heading for Nebraska. Before leaving, they were taken on a brief tour of the city in a Packard. The pair turned down an offer to tour the nearly complete Union Station and were instead taken through the Country Club and Sunset Hill districts. The pair also traveled through Penn Valley Park – where the Bank would open its new headquarters in 2008 – before returning to their train.

At the time of their departure, newspaper accounts indicate both men were in good moods. McAdoo's high spirits were even noted by his secretary, George Cooksey, in a comment to a reporter referencing a recent illness suffered by McAdoo that delayed the hearing schedule.

"Secretary McAdoo seems to be feeling better than he has for two weeks," Cooksey said. "He must have caught the Kansas City spirit."

Kansas Citians were feeling good as well.

"Even if Kansas City does not get a Bank, we know we did our best and showed the Committee the wonderful resources of Kansas City," E.F. Swinney, president of the First National Bank, told a reporter.

"Kansas brains and Kansas men have made Kansas City. This is a Kansas city and you can't beat it."

Others were certainly more optimistic.

At the Clearing House dinner, which was held despite the Committee's departure, several attendees made speeches, *The Times* reported, that "declared there was no doubt but Kansas City would be selected."

2. The cooperative tone seen in Kansas City may have been found only on the West Coast where bankers from other communities offered strong support for a San Francisco Bank, instead of one in Los Angeles, Portland or Seattle. "We have committed ourselves to San Francisco as the location for the regional Bank because we believe that our interest, as well as those of the entire Pacific Coast, which are interknit, will be best served by that location," J.E. Fishburn, president of the Los Angeles Clearing House Association, told the Committee during its L.A. stop.

COMPETITION

Two other cities in what would become the Tenth Federal Reserve District received visits from the Reserve Bank Organizing Committee. A third city, Lincoln, Neb., also submitted a proposal, but did not host a hearing.

How It Looks Now

Drawn for The Bee by Powell.

Omaha felt like it had put itself in a strong position to win one of the regional Reserve Banks, evidenced by a cartoon from the Jan. 27, 1914 edition of The Omaha Bee.

After leaving Kansas City, the committee moved on to Omaha – another of several late additions to the Committee's itinerary. The banks of Omaha and South Omaha suggested a Reserve District encompassing western Iowa; southern South Dakota; a northern tier of Kansas, stopping just short of Kansas City; as well as all of Nebraska, Montana, Idaho, Wyoming, Colorado and Utah.

In the presentation, the Omaha bankers presented a case for their community, and also suggested both Minneapolis-St. Paul and Kansas City might serve as Reserve Bank cities because of the substantial amount of river traffic in the region.

Denver was the next stop on the Committee tour. The city made its bid for a Reserve Bank with a presentation based on the assumption that there would be only eight regional Reserve Banks, and seven of those locations likely were already determined: Boston; New York; Chicago; St. Louis; New Orleans; "a city within the triangle formed by a line drawn from Atlanta to Philadelphia, thence to Cincinnati, and thence to Atlanta;" and, on the Pacific Coast, "presumably San Francisco." For the eighth bank, the Denver contingent suggested a massive district with Denver as its regional headquarters.

The proposed district was bounded on the east by the 100th meridian that bisects Nebraska and cuts south across western Kansas.

"(F)or close to such a line there is a broad belt of country where the density of population is the lightest and where the kind of crops and methods of farming change, where the customary course of business changes, where, with the change of time from 'Central Time' to 'Mountain Time,' the people gradually change their sympathies," reads the presentation from the Denver Chamber of Commerce and the Denver Clearing House Association.

"…With the change of time from 'Central Time' to 'Mountain Time', the people gradually change their sympathies."

For the western edge of its proposed district, the Denver contingent suggested a line near the eastern boundaries of Washington and Oregon. The proposed district would have spanned nearly 1,200 miles from north to south, covering the country from Canada to Mexico.

The Denver presenters, however, apparently feared their proposed region did not include enough financial institutions to meet a key requirement of a regional Bank involving the purchase of stock by member banks to meet minimum capital requirements. The regional Reserve Banks are owned by commercial banks that are required to purchase stock in the regional Bank to become a member of the Federal Reserve System. Although the stock is not publicly traded or available for purchase by individual investors, the Denver contingent provided the Committee with a list of more than 100 individuals willing to purchase stock, some of them agreeing to spend as much as $25,000, to generate a total of nearly $500,000.

Unexpectedly, the Denver hearing revealed some support in the West for a regional Reserve Bank in Kansas City. Although all favored Denver, nearly all speakers told the Committee that Kansas City would be their second choice. Among those saying Kansas City was a suitable backup was Gordon Jones, president of Denver's U.S. National Bank. Jones, who was the lead presenter of Denver's case to the Committee, later became a member of the Federal Reserve Bank of Kansas City's first Board of Directors.

C.N. Blackwell, a New Mexico banker who came to the Committee to voice support for Denver, responded to Committee questions about his part of the country by admitting that the railroads did make Kansas City more accessible to some areas of his state than Denver.

The Denver hearing had a somewhat rushed and odd conclusion. Houston and McAdoo, needing to catch the 4:40 p.m. train that would take them to Seattle, wrapped things up quickly, hearing from only 12 of a planned 25 witnesses. The exchanges with the final two Denver speakers – W.J. Lloyd, a representative of a telegraph company, who was followed by Lucian C. Allen, a telephone company representative – were taken by some Kansas Citians as a sign their city would win the Reserve Bank.

"You have telegraph connections with Kansas City, have you not?" McAdoo asked the telegraph company's representative.

When Lloyd responded that they did, McAdoo asked his next question.

"If a Bank were located in Kansas City and a Branch in Denver, it would be no trouble for them to communicate?" the Treasury Secretary asked.

"None whatever," Lloyd responded.

Allen faced the same line of questioning related to the availability of telephone technology.

The fight to win one of the regional Reserve Banks started almost as soon as President Woodrow Wilson signed the Federal Reserve Act. Many newspapers published editorial cartoons similar to this one from the Dec. 27, 1913 edition of The Omaha World-Herald.

A Final Push

Although the Kansas City contingent felt it had done much to win over the Committee during the Jan. 23 presentation, the group decided to send a three-man contingent to Washington, D.C., in February to secure the support of the Committee's third member, newly appointed Comptroller of the Currency John Skelton Williams, who was not in Kansas City for the hearing.

Thralls, Neal and William T. Kemper, chairman of the National Bank of Commerce and the Commerce Trust Company, spent what Worley called an eventful week in Washington where they met twice with Williams.

"Their first reception in the Comptroller's office was so cool that one of the Committee members afterward remarked that he knew just how Commander Peary felt during his conquest of the North Pole," Worley writes. "All the arguments they were enabled to advance have appeared to have little effect … and they virtually retired under fire from the first session."

The trio turned to Senator Reed and Kansas City Congressman Borland for assistance. Worley writes that, as a favor to Treasury Secretary McAdoo, Reed had interceded on the behalf of Comptroller Williams when Williams' appointment was stalled in the Senate. This created an inroad to Treasury officials for the Kansas City group. Borland, meanwhile, would be instrumental in gaining the Kansas City contingent a crucial second meeting with Williams.

There was also a late appeal to the White House by Reed and Sen. Robert Owen, the Oklahoman who sponsored the Federal Reserve Act. According to a newswire service story, the two men met with President Wilson on March 26 to discuss Kansas City's merits as a Bank site. It is unclear what impact, if any, their appeal had on the Committee's decision. According to the article, Reed also used the meeting to urge Wilson's support for the selection of Kansas City banker J.T. Johnson to the Federal Reserve Board. Johnson was not named to the position.

In the days leading up to the Committee's announcement, it is clear that national opinion about Kansas City had changed dramatically in only three months' time. Newspaper articles attempting to

The third member of the Reserve Bank Organizing Committee, Comptroller of the Currency John Skelton Williams, did not attend many of the Reserve Bank Organizing Committee hearings held throughout the country as his appointment to the position was tied up in the Senate. With Williams not in Kansas City for the hearing, Kansas Citians went to Washington to make their pitch to him.

Missouri Sen. James A. Reed and Oklahoma Sen. Robert L. Owen both worked on behalf of Kansas City's bid to win one of the regional Reserve Banks.

predict the Committee's likely selections, including some that relied on unnamed sources supposedly involved in the process, focused primarily on the question of whether the Committee would pick New Orleans or Atlanta in the Southeast, or Houston or Dallas in Texas. In these stories, there was no doubt that Kansas City would receive a Bank; the only question was the size of its District.

In a March 30, 1914 column, a *Washington Post* columnist, writing under the single-name byline "Holland," looked at the cities under consideration.

"Kansas City would not have been deemed of commercial or financial importance sufficient to justify the establishment there of one of the Federal Reserve Banks had the present law been put upon the statue books, say, in 1894," Holland wrote. "In 1902, the men of finance in New York spoke, occasionally of a rapid growth of Kansas City as a commercial center, and of the accumulation there of funds in large amounts. The yearly reports of clearing-house transactions throughout the United States have invariably told the story of the steady and consistent growth of Kansas City."

THE DECISION

When it came time to determine the Districts, major population centers such as New York, Chicago and St. Louis were already serving as Reserve cities in the national banking system. To some degree, the Committee's challenge was then to fill in the rest of the nation after making allotments for these cities.

In its report, the Reserve Bank Organizing Committee spelled out the criteria used as a basis for their decisions:

- The ability of the member banks within the District to provide the minimum capital of $4 million required for each Reserve Bank by law.

- Mercantile, industrial and financial connections existing within each District.

- The probable ability of the Reserve Bank in each District to meet the demands placed upon it.

- The fair and equitable division of available capital among the Districts.

- Geographical factors including transportation lines and communication facilities.

- The population, area and prevalent business activities of the District.

"In determining the several Districts, the Committee has endeavored to follow state lines as closely as practicable, and wherever it has been found necessary to deviate the division has been along lines which are believed to be most convenient and advantageous for the District affected."

Of the plans presented in Denver, Kansas City and Omaha, the eventual Tenth Federal Reserve District would most closely resemble the District presented by the Kansas City group.

"The region in the middle and far West presented problems of difficulty," the Committee wrote. "Careful consideration was given to the claims of Omaha, Lincoln, Denver and Kansas City, which conflicted in this region."

The committee also pointed to the poll of national banks, where Kansas City received strong support.

In the area that would eventually become the Tenth Federal Reserve District, Kansas City was the top vote-getter with 355 first-place votes, followed by Omaha with 191 and Denver with 132. [3]

> *"Careful consideration was given to the claims of Omaha, Lincoln, Denver and Kansas City, which conflicted in this region."*

---

3. Without any Federal Reserve District boundaries yet determined, Kansas City also received votes from bankers in Arizona, Arkansas and Texas.

THE FEDERAL RESERVE BANKS

12 DISTRICTS

- *First District*: BOSTON
- *Second District*: NEW YORK
- *Third District*: PHILADELPHIA
- *Fourth District*: CLEVELAND

- *Fifth District*: RICHMOND
- *Sixth District*: ATLANTA
- *Seventh District*: CHICAGO
- *Eighth District*: ST. LOUIS

- *Ninth District*: MINNEAPOLIS
- *Tenth District*: KANSAS CITY
- *Eleventh District*: DALLAS
- *Twelfth District*: SAN FRANCISCO

In the Show-Me State, Kansas City received first-place votes from 64 Missouri bankers, compared to 47 for St. Louis.

Looking at individual District states, as was noted during the hearing in Kansas City, support was especially strong in Kansas and Oklahoma.

Of 198 voting Kansas banks, 179 gave first-place votes to Kansas City, Mo.; nine first-place votes signified either Kansas City, Kan. or Mo. as their choice and eight were for simply "Kansas City." Wichita received the remaining two votes.

Chicago		6	65
Dallas	17	11	47
Des Moines			1
Fort Worth	1	2	7
Houston			2
Kansas City	202	63	9
Memphis			1
Muskogee			1
New Orleans			1
Oklahoma	3	8	15
Omaha			1
Philadelphia			1
St. Joseph			1
St. Louis	57	169	31
Tulsa			4
Wichita	1	3	1
St. Louis or Kansas City	1		
St. Louis or Dallas		1	
Dallas or Fort Worth	1		
Total	283	202	101

In Oklahoma, Kansas City received 202 out of 283 first-place votes that were cast.

Although the Districts proposed by those seeking Banks for Denver and Omaha found local support, the proposed Federal Reserve Districts outlined in both of their presentations encompassed regions that did not support the cities, according to the national bank polls. Denver proposed a District that included regions that preferred to be a part of a San Francisco Federal Reserve Bank, while some areas identified for inclusion in a possible Omaha-based Federal Reserve Bank favored Reserve Banks in Minneapolis or Chicago.

"It seemed impossible to serve the great section from Kansas City to the mountains in any other way than by creating a District with Kansas City as the headquarters," the Committee said in a statement issued a few days after it announced the 12 Reserve Bank locations. "The Kansas City banks serve a very distinctive territory, and will serve it more satisfactorily than St. Louis could have done."

The Committee went on to note that the relations of the Tenth Federal Reserve District "are much more largely with Kansas City" than any other city in the nation's midsection, adding that Kansas City was the region's "dominant banking and business center."

Although Kansas City had made a strong case throughout the process, it was the second meeting with Comptroller Williams that likely clinched the Bank for the city.

Worley writes colorfully in describing that second meeting:

"Summing up their forces for the final attack, this (Kansas City) committee moved up its heavy

When asked to vote for their top three choices for a city that would be home to their regional Reserve Bank, Oklahoma bankers strongly supported Kansas City. Results from the votes were included in the Reserve Bank Organizing Committee's final report.

P.W. Goebel, president of the Kansas City Clearing House, was one of several local business leaders who worked for Kansas City's Reserve Bank bid. Goebel, a Kansas banker who had served in the Kansas Legislature and been president of the Kansas Bankers Association, later became president of the American Bankers Association.

artillery and backed it up with machine gunfire that was so rapid it did not allow the Comptroller time to assert and propound his own theories."

When it came time to make the decision, all three members of the Reserve Bank Organizing Committee supported locating a Bank in Kansas City.

An unpublished 1914 report by Willis that is the focal point for a paper written in 2001 by University of Hawaii Economics Professor David Hammes suggests that a regional Federal Reserve Bank for the central United States would have been feasible in Denver or even Fort Worth.

But Willis wrote that "the adoption of such a plan would imply a reversal of the normal course of business which … is toward the north and east, and would compel various cities which have been in the habit of acting as reserve holders for others to invert this relationship. It is not believed, therefore, that so drastic a change should be made, but that the headquarters chosen should be in the northern and eastern portion of the District."

Kansas City residents might wonder why the local contingent chose to rally in support of Kansas City, Mo., which faced a suitable cross-state rival, instead of Kansas City, Kan., which might have had an easier road to winning a Reserve Bank by virtue of being conveniently located across the state line.

The issue of two Reserve Banks in Missouri was raised during the Kansas City hearing by Houston. According to newspaper accounts, P.W. Goebel, president of the Kansas City Clearing House, responded that he would be happy with a Reserve Bank on the Kansas side of the state line, but that a Kansas Bank would be only "next best" to having the Bank in Missouri.

The entire region was clearly united in the effort. Although Goebel was born in Germany, he had lived in Kansas for four decades, during which he was a successful Kansas banker, served two terms in the Kansas Legislature and had been president of the Kansas Bankers Association. He would later go on to become president of the American Bankers Association.

The breadth of the support was also evident outside of the hearing room. A Jan. 14, 1915 letter to the Committee from the Kansas Bankers Association supported Kansas City, Mo.:

"As a matter of provincial state pride, it will mean as much to the state of Kansas as if some city within her own border were designated, for essentially Kansas City is our city."

Hammes' paper suggests that Kansas City, Mo., may have won the local support, in part, because work was nearing completion on the massive Union Station. Perhaps fittingly, the station today is one of the Federal Reserve Bank's neighbors.

Coincidentally, an article about the Bank's opening in the Nov. 16, 1914 edition of *The Kansas City Star* also made a connection to the train station:

"A $6 million Union Station with about $50 million for terminals built by the railroads, officially established Kansas City as the gateway or center for the transportation lines of the West and Southwest, and now the Bank officially establishes it as the center for the business and financial lines."

A connection to Union Station was also made by a man who would soon find himself leading the effort to establish the Bank. Jo Zach Miller, Jr., who was at that time vice president at Commerce Trust Company, offered a lengthy comment for the April 3, 1914 edition of *The Kansas City Times*:

"The placing of the Federal Reserve Bank here is as great (a) benefit to Kansas City as the new Union Depot. It will center the attention of 5,200 banks on Kansas City. I believe it will concentrate the principal reserve of the cities of the Southwest to banks here.

"…It is one of the greatest boons that could possibly come to Kansas City. It turns the eyes of the whole Southwest more and more to Kansas City as the financial and trading center."

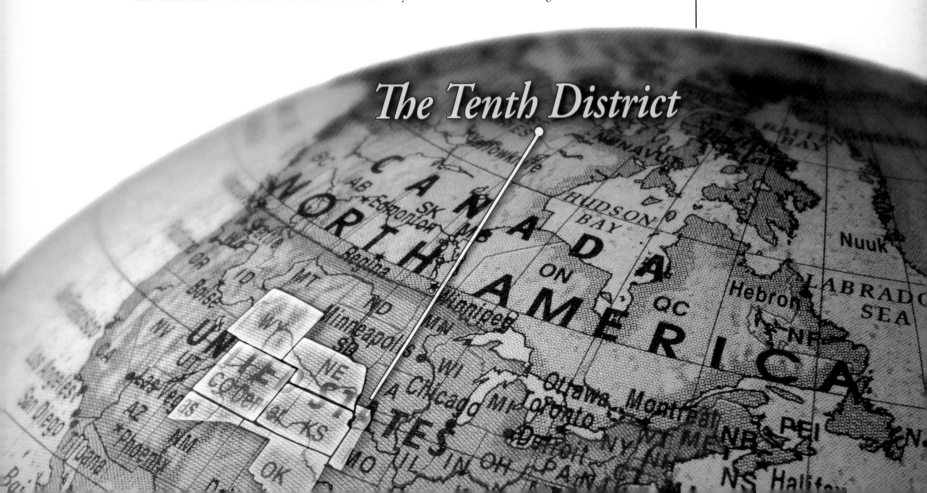

The Tenth District

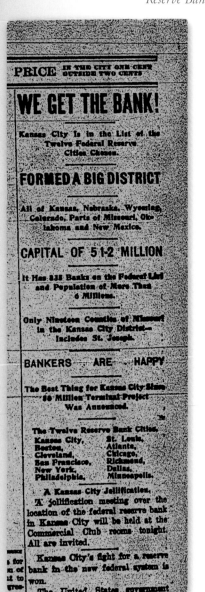

CELEBRATION

The decision, announced on April 2, 1914, was celebrated in Kansas City.

The Kansas City Star's April 3, 1914 edition quoted Goebel as saying the decision was "triumphant proof of Kansas City's business importance."

Similar comments were made by the city's bankers.

"This is such a big event for Kansas City that we can't settle down to do our work this morning," J.F. Downing, president of Kansas City's New England National Bank, told *The Star*. "All of us are inclined to go visiting and exchange congratulations and felicitations. It's a great achievement to build up a commerce that warranted and virtually demanded such a decision from the Organizing Committee."

Local newspapers commended the effort, *"I don't want to talk, I want to sing."* both of those in the city and those in the neighboring communities who offered their support.

"The victory is not Kansas City's alone," *The Kansas City Journal* wrote in an April 4, 1914 editorial. "It is a victory for that wide area wherein lie the contributing elements of Kansas City's greatness. Almost without exception, the smaller banks in this territory came loyally to the front and did their part in achieving the result. The success of the effort will bind together more closely than ever all of the thriving cities, towns and rural communities in a District comprising more than half a million square miles and containing more than six million people."

A "jollification meeting" to celebrate the decision was quickly planned for April 3 in the Commercial Club Rooms of the Kansas City Board of Trade building. According to newspaper accounts, the event featured a band, professional singers, a performer dressed as Uncle Sam and three hours of speeches by local bankers and elected officials including Sen. Reed and Congressman Borland, who called the decision the biggest victory in Kansas City history.

The event was "a meeting of happy faces, wreathed in smiles," according to *The Times*. The spirit of the event might have been best expressed by Kemper, who, when called upon to speak to the group, responded, "I don't want to talk, I want to sing."

The Kansas City Journal proclaimed the city's selection on its April 3, 1914 front page.

INCORPORATION

To establish the Banks, the Reserve Bank Organizing Committee selected five banks from each District to sign the Banks' certificates of incorporation.

In Kansas City, the group met in the second-story offices of the Kansas City Clearing House, across the street from the Fidelity Trust Company Building and its bell tower. In its May 18, 1914 edition, *The Kansas City Star* wrote somewhat dramatically about the meeting, noting that as the bell tolled, Thralls, who had been selected the group's secretary, rose and spoke:

"Gentlemen, you hear the clock tolling the hour of noon, the time fixed at Washington for the transaction of this business. Shall we begin?"

The Fidelity National Bank & Trust Co., which stood at the corner of Ninth and Walnut St. When the building's bell tower tolled noon, bankers meeting in a nearby building started signing the papers that officially incorporated the Federal Reserve Bank of Kansas City.

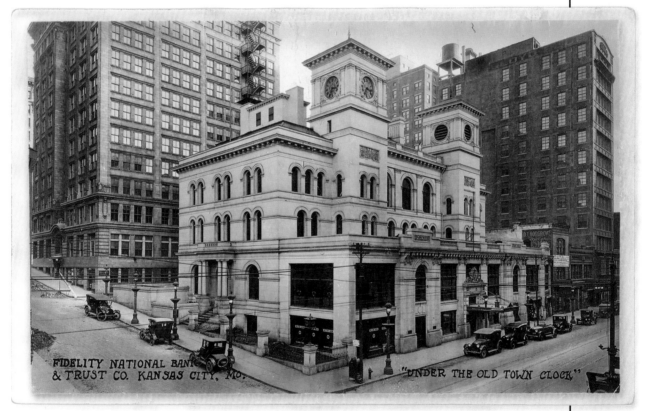

FIDELITY NATIONAL BANK & TRUST CO. KANSAS CITY, MO.   "UNDER THE OLD TOWN CLOCK"

Two individuals from each financial institution signed the document and attached their corporate seal. They were:

- J.C. Mitchell, president, and E.I. Irish, cashier, Denver National Bank;
- P.L. Hall, president, and Samuel Patterson, cashier, Central National Bank, Lincoln, Neb.;
- V.B. Caldwell, vice president, and W.E. Rhoades, cashier, United States National Bank, Omaha, Neb.;

- William Daley, president, and J.A. Rendle, cashier, Rawlins National Bank, Rawlins, Wyo.;

- Asa E. Ramsay, vice president, and L.W. Duncan, cashier, First National Bank, Muskogee, Okla.

After the ceremony, the group attended a luncheon, where the bankers told reporters that their counterparts back home did not resent Kansas City's success in winning the regional Reserve Bank headquarters.

"The people of my city did everything in their power to land the big proposition, but since we have lost, we extend our hand gladly to the big city that won," Lincoln, Neb. banker Hall told *The Kansas City Journal*.

Mitchell, the Denver banker, told a reporter from *The Kansas City Post*, that Denver bankers hated to lose, but were ready to work with Kansas City. He also made a few comments about the Federal Reserve Act.

"When this bill begins its actual work, you will see a big difference in business conditions," Mitchell said. "Already confidence is being restored as it is becoming generally known that the day of money panics is over."

"Already Confidence is being restored as it is becoming generally known that the day of money panics is over."

Preparing *for* opening

The Federal Reserve has a unique public-private structure. The Board of Governors in Washington, D.C., which has broad oversight responsibilities for the entire Federal Reserve System, is a governmental agency. The regional Banks are private corporations with their own Boards of Directors. These directors are a unique mix – six of the nine directors are elected by commercial banks that are members of the Federal Reserve System in each District, while the remaining three positions are appointees of the Board of Governors.

This blend of positions continues to serve the System well, but in 1914, it was a cause of some delay.

Each Board of Directors had its six elected directors in place thanks to a process that started after the certificate of incorporation signing. Filling the three appointed positions, however, could not begin until the Board of Governors of the Federal Reserve System was sworn in on Aug. 10, 1914.[4] The Governors quickly turned to the task of filling the regional Bank Boards. The first annual report issued by

4. Because no two members of the Board of Governors can come from the same Federal Reserve District, the selection of the initial members of the Board of Governors could not begin until after the boundaries for the Reserve Districts were determined.

The First
Board of Directors
of THE FEDERAL RESERVE BANK *of* KANSAS CITY

From left: Jo Zach Miller, Jr.; Thomas C. Byrne; Willis J. Bailey; Meade L. McClure; R.H. Malone; Charles M. Sawyer; Asa E. Ramsay; L.A. Wilson; C.E. Burnham; and Gordon Jones.

THE BANK'S FIRST BOARD OF DIRECTORS INCLUDED REPRESENTATIVES
from THROUGHOUT THE TENTH FEDERAL RESERVE DISTRICT.

JO ZACH MILLER, JR., Kansas City, Mo., *chairman**

ASA E. RAMSAY, Muskogee, Okla., *vice chairman**

R.H. MALONE, *personal business in investments,* Denver, Colo.

THOMAS C. BYRNE, *president,* Bryne & Hammer Dry Goods Company, Omaha, Neb.

MEADE L. MCCLURE, *president,* Drumm Livestock Commission Company, Kansas City, Mo.

L.A. WILSON, *personal business in loans and investments,* El Reno, Okla.

GORDON JONES, *president,* U.S. National Bank, Denver, Colo.

WILLIS J. BAILEY, *president,* Exchange National Bank, Atchison, Kan.

C.E. BURNHAM, *president,* Norfolk National Bank, Norfolk, Neb.

The Bank's first governor, Charles Sawyer, is also pictured.

*The chairman and vice chairman were paid positions on the Bank's staff in 1914.

THE FIRST
employees

Auditor M.J. McNellis on opening day, November 16, 1914.

The Federal Reserve Bank of Kansas City's first two employees ended up on dramatically different courses, with one's career cut tragically short while the other climbed rapidly through the ranks of the central bank.

The hiring of R.P. Ritter was among the first tasks completed by Bank Chairman Jo Zach Miller, Jr., coming before the Bank's Board had done much in the way of preparing for the Bank opening.

Miller hired Ritter after being told by a Kansas City businessman that the young Kansas Citian was "worth $500 a month as a secretary but would work for $150," according to Jess Worley's unpublished Bank history.

Ritter was hired in October 1914 and remained at the Bank until Aug. 20, 1916, when he became bed-ridden by illness. He died at his Kansas City home on Jan. 15, 1917.

Although little is known about Ritter, Worley wrote more extensively about James Buchanan, Jr., the second employee hired to work at the Bank. Buchanan was "about 18" when he came to Kansas City to find work and went to meet with Miller at the Bank's temporary office in the Commerce Building.

It was a short meeting, but Miller discovered that the young man was the nephew of a former academic rival from Miller's days at St. Louis University some 30 years prior. Miller and the elder Buchanan finished school with the same final grades and the same number of academic honors.

Miller later said that the difference between himself and the elder Buchanan was that Buchanan "never seemed to have to study his lessons, while I used most of the recess periods, play hours and holidays in getting mine, and that I couldn't, for the life of me, see why I couldn't surpass him with the amount of work I was doing."

The younger Buchanan was also apparently a good student, working at the Bank for only a few years before going to work for the Federal Reserve Board in Washington, D.C. By the early 1920s, he held a senior position in the examining department.

In the days before its opening, the Federal Reserve Bank of Kansas City employed only a handful of workers, mostly in clerical positions, before opening for business with a full staff of 14 employees.

The opening day employees were:

- R.P. RITTER, *secretary to the chairman and temporary secretary to the Board of Directors*
- JAMES BUCHANAN, JR., *clerk*
- JENNIE BURRIS, *stenographer*
- R.E. CONDON, *clerk*
- KATHERINE DALTON, *stenographer*
- CHARLES FERGUSON, *teller*
- MARGUERITE KLUMP, *stenographer*
- E.D. MCALLISTER, *teller*
- RUBY RAINE, *stenographer*
- CLEO UMSTEAD, *stenographer*
- E.P. TYNER, *general bookkeeper*
- W.M. GAMBLE, *porter*
- J.W. MCBRIDE, *watchman*
- M.J. MCNELLIS, *auditor*

McNellis was the highest paid among them at $208.34 a month, while Gamble earned the least at $50.00 per month as porter.

the Board of Governors offers some details on the process. Specifically, it notes that the Board was especially careful because one of the appointed positions on each regional Board would be that Bank's chairman of the Board and Federal Reserve agent.

"The office is undoubtedly one which calls for exceptional qualifications and is therefore difficult to fill," the Board said in the 1914 annual report. It also states a Reserve Bank chairman must be a person of "solidity, independence and tried character."

To find these individuals, the Board "deemed it essential to scrutinize every name submitted for appointment or suggested from any source" through a process which "required time and necessitated visits by members of the Board to various and distant parts of the country, as well as the invitation of competent advisers to Washington for consultation."

The Board completed its selections and announced the appointments in early October.

In Kansas City, a local newspaper account of the announcement noted that it came after "a long period of anxious waiting."

Jo Zach Miller, Jr., a 51-year-old vice president of Commerce Trust Company, was selected as the Kansas City Bank's first chairman, a choice that drew praise from the local media.

"Kansas City is highly pleased at the appointment of Mr. Miller," reads one newspaper account. "He is regarded as an excellent choice for this very important place and it is gratifying that he can see his way clear to accept the responsibility."

The story goes on to point out that Miller's pay of $7,500 annually was relatively minimal when compared against his banker's salary:

"Only a worthy desire to be of patriotic service can justify such a sacrifice. And the people of District No. 10 are fortunate in having such a man available for this service."

With Miller's selection completing the Board of Directors, the reporter noted that "nothing now remains except to start the machinery going."

Jo Zach Miller, Jr., a 51-year-old vice president of Commerce Trust Company was chosen as the first chairman of the Federal Reserve Bank of Kansas City. Miller's leadership and vision would be key factors in establishing the new regional Reserve Bank.

J.Z. Miller, Jr.

The first Board of Directors meeting

The Board of Directors of the Federal Reserve Bank of Kansas City met for the first time on a Friday afternoon, Oct. 16, 1914, in the board room of the Commerce Trust Company building in downtown Kansas City.

The first meeting lasted a little more than three hours, during which the directors prepared for an Oct. 20 meeting in Washington, D.C., by reviewing a list of questions received from the Board of Governors relating to numerous operating issues. The directors decided the Federal Reserve Bank of Kansas City could be open in less than one month, by Nov. 15, and could use temporary quarters in the Commerce Building. At this first meeting, the directors also chose Charles M. Sawyer, 48, as the Bank's first governor – a title that would later be replaced by the position of Bank president under the Banking Act of 1935.

Worley's history includes a partial transcript of the first meeting, including comments that offer insight to the hurried schedule under which the entire Federal Reserve System was operating.

Miller, who would later serve as governor after it became clear what duties each job would entail, talked about being notified of his selection while at his ranch in Texas. He told his fellow directors that, after receiving a telegram regarding his selection, he departed the ranch "within two or three hours," on his way to Washington, D.C., to begin his new position with two days of meetings.

The first meeting of the Federal Reserve Bank of Kansas City's Board of Directors was on Oct. 16, 1914. In attendance: Jo Zach Miller, Jr.; Gordon Jones; R.H. Malone; L.A. Wilson; Thomas C. Byrne; Asa E. Ramsay; and Willis J. Bailey. Records indicate Director Meade L. McClure also attended the meeting, but was not photographed for unknown reasons. Director C.E. Burnham did not attend the meeting.

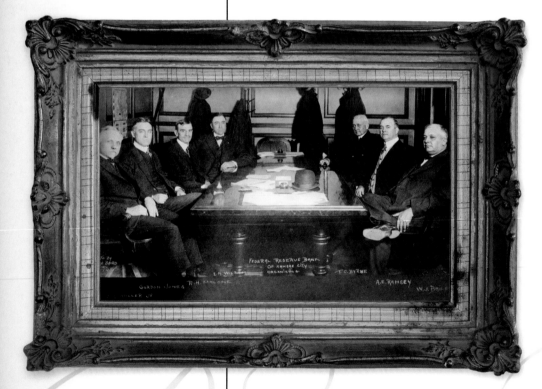

THE FIRST MEMBER BANK

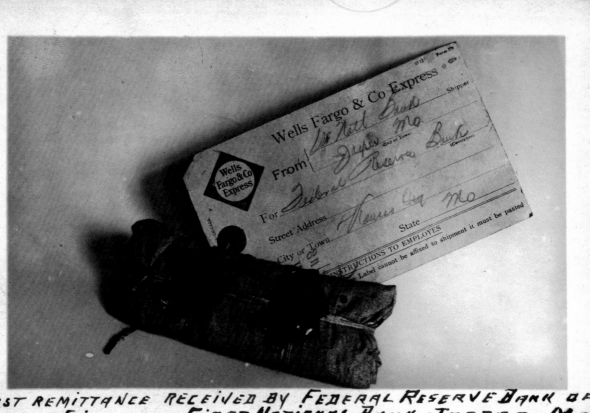

FIRST REMITTANCE RECEIVED BY FEDERAL RESERVE BANK OF KANSAS CITY FROM FIRST NATIONAL BANK, JASPER, Mo. NOVEMBER 2, 1914.

Commercial banks chartered by the federal government and state banks that choose the designation are known as Federal Reserve member banks.

The designation has several implications for the individual commercial banks, including the determination of their regulatory agency.

To become a member, the commercial bank must purchase stock in their regional Federal Reserve Bank in an amount equal to 6 percent of their capital and surplus, half of which must be paid while the other half is subject to call by the Board of Governors of the Federal Reserve System. The Federal Reserve stock does not carry with it the control and financial interest of common stock in publicly held companies, and the stock may not

be sold or pledged as collateral for loans. Member banks receive a 6 percent dividend on the stock and the right to vote in specific director elections.

The Federal Reserve Bank of Kansas City received its first subscription payment more than two weeks before it was open for business.

The First National Bank of Jasper, Mo., sent the Federal Reserve Bank $350 in gold as its first payment – 1 percent of the commercial bank's capital and surplus of $35,000.

"The Jasper bank is a little ahead of time, because we have not started yet, but we shall find a place to put the money until the Bank opens," Chairman Jo Zach Miller, Jr., told a reporter. "We won't send it back."

THE R.A. LONG BUILDING

At 16 stories, the R.A. Long Building is sometimes referred to as Kansas City's first skyscraper.

The building that served as the first home of the Federal Reserve Bank of Kansas City was built downtown in 1906 for $1.125 million by R.A. Long to house his Long-Bell Lumber Company.

Both Long, and the building's architect, Henry F. Hoit, have deep ties to the community with legacies that are evident even today.

Long's mansion, Corinthian Hall, sometimes described as the "palace on Gladstone Boulevard," houses the Kansas City Museum and his country estate was Longview Farm, in suburban Lee's Summit, Mo. Long's family donated the land that became Longview Community College and sold other properties that today are Longview Lake and nearby residential areas. Long was involved in several notable community efforts, but he may be most well-known in Kansas City today as the man who led the drive to build Liberty Memorial.

Hoit, meanwhile, designed several of Kansas City's most prominent structures, including the Kansas City Power and Light Building. Hoit also was on a team that submitted a rejected design for Liberty Memorial. The design featured a giant obelisk at the extreme south end of the current memorial site – a plan that would have placed the tower immediately across the street from the Bank's current front lawn.

The R.A. Long building on the northwest corner of 10th and Grand Streets, circa 1910.

Opening Day

The Bank's Board of Directors held its second meeting on Halloween morning, starting with a tour of two of the five downtown Kansas City buildings under consideration as the Bank headquarters.

The five buildings were:

- The Kansas City Southern Railway Building, northeast corner of 11th and Walnut streets;
- The United States and Mexican Trust Company location in the Bryant Building, southwest corner of 11th Street and Grand Avenue;
- The Fidelity Trust Company, on the southeast corner of Ninth and Walnut Streets.
- The New York Life Insurance Building at Ninth and Baltimore streets;
- The ground floor of the R.A. Long Building at the northwest corner of 10th Street and Grand Avenue.

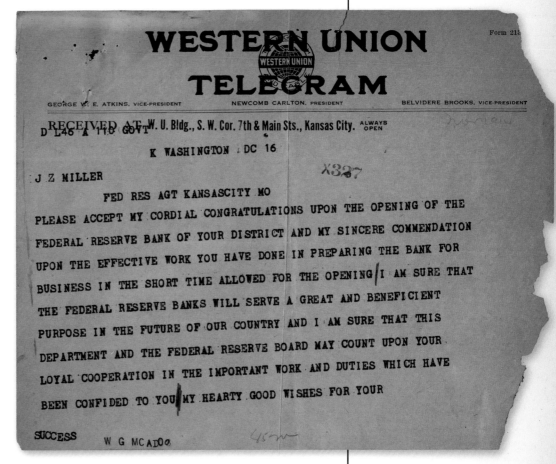

The telegram from Treasury Secretary William McAdoo to Jo Zach Miller, Jr., congratulating the Bank on a successful opening.

They chose the ground floor of the Long Building, directly across the street from where the Bank would begin constructing a new headquarters in 1920. The Bank paid $7,500 annually to lease about 8,500 square feet, primarily on the building's main floor, but also including a filing room on the building's 15th floor.

Newspaper accounts of the selection note that the Long Building's large marble lobby, including a fountain in the center, had been designed to house a bank. In fact, the leases of lobby tenants – including private offices, a historical association and a cigar stand – all contained a unique provision

THE FIRST WORLD WAR

Today, the Federal Reserve Bank of Kansas City's headquarters is neighbor to the city's monument for those who served in the first World War. But, the connections between the nation's central bank and "the war to end all wars" extend far beyond the proximity to Liberty Memorial.

In fact, preparations for opening the central bank and the war converge at a single point in history. With war erupting across Europe, on Aug. 10, 1914, the first governors of the Federal Reserve System were administered the oath of office.

Although the United States would not enter the fighting until the spring of 1917, the war had an impact on the country and on efforts to prepare the central bank for opening.

The issue is among the first addressed in the Federal Reserve Board's inaugural annual report:

"Seldom, if ever, has the banking and business community of the country found itself in a situation of such uncertainty and perplexity. The outbreak of hostilities in Europe led immediately to a serious rupture of international financial relationships, not only in the affected areas of Europe, but throughout the whole commercial world. The United States was directly and profoundly affected by the suspension of communication with Europe, involving as its most serious consequences the temporary breaking down of the export trade and the collapse of the financial markets, with resulting shock to the credit system."

The fighting had wide financial implications, among the most dramatic was on the cotton market.

In the early 1900s, about 60 percent of the U.S. cotton crop was sent overseas, making Europe a crucial market for cotton producers. In 1914, U.S. cotton farmers planted more acres than usual and, after a favorable growing season, a large crop was nearing harvest. The Board's report notes that,

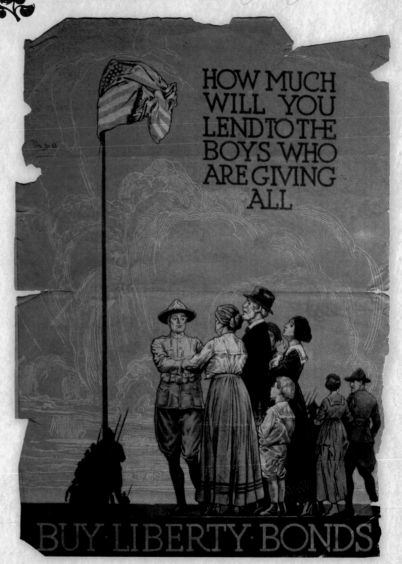

HOW MUCH WILL YOU LEND TO THE BOYS WHO ARE GIVING ALL

BUY LIBERTY BONDS

even without the war, the situation would have led to depressed cotton prices. The situation, however, was worsened by the closing of cotton exchanges in both the United States and England.

Cotton farmers, who were largely credit-dependent, were unable to sell their crops – causing concern for bankers in cotton-producing states. The potential for widespread banking problems made it even more important for the new central bank to open quickly.

Federal Reserve Bank of Kansas City Chairman Jo Zach Miller, Jr., talked with a reporter about the need to expedite the System-wide opening, after returning from a meeting in Washington, D.C.

"The cotton situation is one of the gravest in the history of this country," Miller told the newspaper reporter. "Here in Kansas City we have little to do with cotton and we do not realize how it is woven into the economics of the entire South. It affects not only the farmer, but the whole commercial fabric of the South. When cotton is ill, the whole South is abed. The retail merchant cannot be paid and he, in turn, cannot pay the wholesaler and the banker cannot lend any more money."

Eventually, Treasury Secretary William McAdoo selected an opening date of Nov. 16, 1914 - sooner, even, than the originally scheduled opening date of Dec. 1.

"I am impelled to this decision particularly because of conditions in the South, and the confident belief that the prompt opening of the Reserve Banks will be very helpful to the cotton situation and to general business in all sections of the country," McAdoo said in announcing the date.

In its annual report, the Board said the expedited opening allowed the release of "a large amount of reserve funds, thereby enabling member banks to make new loans and grant extensions (to cotton farmers) which otherwise would have been impossible."

Liberty Bonds and the howitzer

The impact on the opening date was far from the only connection between the war and the Federal Reserve.

The Federal Reserve Bank of Kansas City was extremely active in the Liberty Bond campaigns to raise funding for the war. The initial campaign brought both W.P.G. Harding, governor of the Federal Reserve, and Treasury Secretary McAdoo, who was the creator of the bond campaign, to Kansas City.

"I have the utmost faith in Kansas City - I know it will do its full share in subscribing to the huge Liberty Loan, which will aid in forever establishing liberty and sound the death knell of Prussianism," McAdoo said to those greeting him at Union Station on May 25, 1917.

Kansas Citians, recalling McAdoo's role in the decision to locate a Reserve Bank in the city, warmly welcomed the Treasury secretary during a series of local meetings and a speech at the city's Convention Hall. The stop was one of several McAdoo made to drum up support for the campaign.

The Federal Reserve Bank of Kansas City received a 105-mm German howitzer for its work on the Liberty Bond campaigns. Today, the cannon is on display at the National World War I Museum at Liberty Memorial.

Continued on next page

"Every dollar subscribed to this Liberty Loan is a blow struck for liberty throughout the world, a blow struck for democracy and self-government throughout the world, a blow struck for that happy day when the self-governed peoples of all the nations of the earth will rise up and proclaim the United Sates the greatest apostle of liberty, the noble champion who has brought to them the assurance of that stable and just peace which has been the dream of all the ages," McAdoo told a similar meeting in Chicago a few days before arriving in Kansas City.

Nationwide, the Liberty Bond campaign was extremely successful. It was also successful in the Tenth Federal Reserve District, where the Federal Reserve Bank of Kansas City led the effort. The bond campaign also included many of the same individuals who had been involved in the effort to win a regional Reserve Bank for the city three years earlier.

For its work, the Bank was awarded a 105-mm German howitzer captured by the U.S. 35th Division on Oct. 2, 1918, in the Battle of the Argonne, the final major battle of the war.

The Bank planned to put the cannon in a specially designed room in its new headquarters at 925 Grand. As construction on the building continued, however, Bank officials decided their idea was unfeasible. They instead gave the howitzer, which had been on temporary display outdoors on the north side of the Kansas City Public Library, to Rockhurst College. The presentation was made during a Nov. 2, 1921 visit to the college by Marshall Ferdinand Foch, the supreme commander of the allied armies. Foch was one of the five allied war leaders, including Gen. John J. Pershing, who were in Kansas City for the dedication of Liberty Memorial the previous day.

At Rockhurst, the cannon often fell prey to college pranks and was regularly pushed down Troost Avenue by students from rival schools. Rockhurst later sold the gun to a Shawnee Mission, Kan. man who put it on display in his yard. In 1977, he donated the cannon to Liberty Memorial and it was finally moved to the Memorial in November 1980. The howitzer is now on display at the National World War I Museum at Liberty Memorial.

Kansas City raised more than $2.5 million for the construction of Liberty Memorial in 1919. The memorial, honoring those who served in the First World War "in defense of liberty and our country" is located across the street from the Bank's headquarters at 1 Memorial Drive.

allowing for termination if the building's owner could lease the space to a bank. Work to both renovate the lobby and relocate tenants started immediately.

The second Board of Directors meeting included decisions about employee salaries and the Bank's Executive Committee, which included directors. The Committee began working continuous day-long sessions the following Monday, Nov. 2, in preparation for the planned Reserve System-wide opening date of Nov. 16.

"This work (by the Executive Committee) comprised a variety of duties including innumerable conferences with businessmen, furniture salesmen, supply salesmen, bank officials and prospective employees; also trips of inspection and inquiry, a great amount of correspondence by letter and wire with the Federal Reserve Board, and an endless amount of exhaustive discussions of letters pertaining to the opening of the Bank," Worley writes. "There was a great amount of urgent work to be done and temporary employees were hired to do this preliminary work."

Two artist renderings of the Federal Reserve Bank of Kansas City's offices in the R.A. Long Building from the Nov. 16, 1914 edition of The Kansas City Star.

The Board of Directors held numerous meetings in the coming days, where they did everything from draw lots to determine office terms, thereby staggering the terms for future elections and appointments, to determining the duties of the Bank's officers and operating rules.

"While the officers and new employees of the Bank were busily engaged in preparing the permanent quarters and installing various systems during the first half of November, the directors were far from idle," Worley writes.

With no vault space immediately available, the Bank instead relied on the vaults of the Commerce Trust Company for several weeks. The Federal Reserve had used space on the second floor of the Commerce building as temporary quarters, and Commerce employees had assisted the Federal Reserve in handling payments of reserves and subscriptions for stock from commercial banks that became members of the Federal Reserve.

KANSAS CITY

THE FEDERAL BANK OPENS

KANSAS CITY THE MONEY CAPITAL OF THE SOUTHWEST.

A Telegram From Secretary McAdoo Formally Started Uncle Sam's Cash Shop Here—Visitors Throng the New Quarters.

The federal reserve bank of district No. 10 opened this morning in the R. A. Long Building, thus officially establishing Kansas City as the commercial and financial capital of a rich territory, including all the states of Kansas, Nebraska, Colorado and Wyoming and parts of Missouri, Oklahoma and New Mexico.

A 6 million-dollar Union Station, with about 50 million dollars for terminals, built by the railroads, officially established Kansas City as the gateway or center for the transportation lines of the West and Southwest, and now the bank officially establishes it as the center for the business and financial lines.

NO FORMAL EXERCISES.

Bankers and business men from all parts of the district attended the birth of the new bank this morning. There were no formal exercises. The nine directors and the officers of the bank simply opened the doors and stood shaking hands and smiling as the hundreds flocked into the building and overran the quarters. Workmen were still busy installing fixtures when porters from the different floral shops came bearing great vases filled with American Beauty roses and chrysanthemums of all colors. The flowers bore cards of congratulations and good wishes from banks and business firms outside as well as within Kansas City.

A telegram from William G. McAdoo, Secretary of the Treasury, to the Federal Reserve Bank authorized the official opening. It read:

Meanwhile, the Bank's quarters in the Long Building had to undergo some changes. Areas had to be enclosed to create secure workrooms, and the Bank paid $1,615 for an alarm system to be operational for the opening day.

Work on building fixtures was still under way on opening day, Nov. 16, 1914, when the Bank received a telegram from Treasury Secretary McAdoo:

"Please accept my cordial congratulations upon the opening of the Federal Reserve Bank of your District, and my sincere commendation upon the effective work you have done in preparing the Bank for business in the short time allowed for the opening. I am sure that the Federal Reserve Banks will serve a great and beneficent purpose in the future of our country, and I am sure that this Department and the Federal Reserve Board count upon your loyal cooperation in the important work and duties which have been confided to you. My hearty good wishes for your success."

The Bank also received telegrams announcing its charter had been executed, allowing it to open for business.

Paul Warburg, a banker and long-time advocate of creating the Federal Reserve who was also a member of the first Federal Reserve Board, said the opening day of the nation's new central bank was the Fourth of July for the nation's economic life.

"The new banking system, wisely administered, will prove to be the means not of inflation, but of safety, independence and gradual healthy expansions. How soon we may become a world power, equal in strength and independence to those on whom we have had to lean until now, will depend upon our ability to avail ourselves of the opportunity now open to us," Warburg told reporters.

In Kansas City, Bank officials expected an opening day with few visitors. It turned out otherwise.

According to Worley's history, much of the first day was spent talking with well-wishers who filed into the building until the close of business. The Bank's officers and directors, he wrote, became a receiving committee, welcoming guests "every moment of the day."

Nov. 16, 1914

In addition to the visitors, there were the more than 500 letters and telegrams, along with flowers and plants, many reflecting that the Kansas City Federal Reserve Bank was a Bank serving the entire Tenth Federal Reserve District.

One newspaper account paints an almost chaotic scene of that first day with a group of local bankers rushing to shake hands with Thralls, who had resigned his post at the Clearing House to accept the job of secretary at the new Reserve Bank. The bankers accidentally overturned a vase of chrysanthemums onto Thralls' desk as they reached to congratulate him – an incident a reporter colorfully described as the new Bank being "baptized … with good Missouri River water."

Opening day of the Federal Reserve Bank of Kansas City. Nov. 16, 1914. Flowers from well-wishers cover the desks of Vice Chairman of the Bank's Board of Directors Asa Ramsay and Chairman Jo Zach Miller, Jr.

Growth

BANK *of* KANSAS CITY

THE NATION'S NEW CENTRAL BANK *was a success.*

In the months after its opening, the Federal Reserve Bank of Kansas City expanded quickly. After starting in 1914 with a relatively small staff working out of the main floor of the R.A. Long Building, in the final months of 1917, the Bank had 250 employees spread throughout five floors of the Long Building and in office space in two other buildings. The lease was set to expire in two years and the Bank's 1917 annual report indicates informal discussions about a new headquarters had begun: "…time has demonstrated that the present quarters are inadequate in space and arrangement."

The discussions became formal on Jan. 10, 1918, when Bank Governor Jo Zach Miller, Jr., proposed a building project to the Bank's Board of Directors.

With vault space also inadequate, and it being impractical to lease additional space, "the Governor urged that immediate steps be taken to provide for a future home for the Bank," Jess Worley wrote in his unpublished Bank history. "The directors unanimously adopted resolutions endorsing the Governor's report and recommendations. This meeting was the beginning of what later became the greatest bank building in the West."

Two weeks later, Bank Directors Harrison W. Gibson and Meade L. McClure, along with Chairman Asa E. Ramsay, were appointed as the Bank's building committee and instructed to investigate possible building sites.

For Consideration

LOCATIONS *for* THE BANK'S NEW HEADQUARTERS

Before deciding to build on the northeast corner of 10th Street and Grand Avenue, leaders of the Federal Reserve Bank of Kansas City gave at least preliminary consideration to 18 locations for the Bank's new headquarters.

In a March 27, 1918 letter to Jo Zach Miller, Jr., Kansas City real estate agent Hughes Bryant discussed each of the sites, noting the benefits and potential drawbacks of many, and suggesting a likely price for each.

The sites:

Southeast corner of 10th and Wyandotte streets

Northeast corner of 10th and Wyandotte streets

Northwest corner of 10th Street and Baltimore Avenue

Northeast corner of 10th and Main streets

Southeast corner of Ninth and Main streets

Southwest corner of Ninth and Walnut streets

Northeast corner of 10th and Walnut streets

Northeast corner of 10th Street and Grand Avenue

Southwest corner of Ninth and McGee streets

Northeast corner of 11th and McGee streets

Southwest corner of 11th and Locust streets

Northeast corner of 11th and Locust streets

Southwest corner of 12th and McGee streets

Northwest corner of 13th and McGee streets

Southeast corner of 14th and McGee streets

Northwest corner of 15th and McGee streets

Southwest corner of 12th and Wyandotte streets

18th Street between Grand Avenue and McGee Street

Although all of these sites would find various uses in the years that followed, several are especially noteworthy:

- The southwest corner of Ninth and McGee streets was eventually turned into a surface parking lot that the Bank purchased for employee parking in 1979.

- The southwest corner of 11th and Locust streets is part of the city block that now houses Kansas City's City Hall, which opened in 1937.

- The northeast corner of 11th and Locust streets is an area that some outside of the Bank supported as a possible location for the Bank's new headquarters when Bank officials were exploring locations prior to choosing 1 Memorial Drive.

- The southeast corner of 14th and McGee streets is in the middle of an area where, in 2007, a new arena opened.

- The northwest corner of 15th and McGee streets is also within the area of the arena. A building on that site might also have been lost to the construction of Interstate 670.

- The southwest corner of 12th and Wyandotte streets is the Barney Allis Plaza.

- The area along 18th Street between Grand and McGee is today divided between a parking lot and the front yard for *The Kansas City Star*. The estate of *Star* founder William Rockhill Nelson was especially aggressive in marketing this site for a possible home for the Bank in 1918. The estate was willing to sell the property to the Bank for $500,000, about $200,000 less than it said it would ask from any other potential buyer.

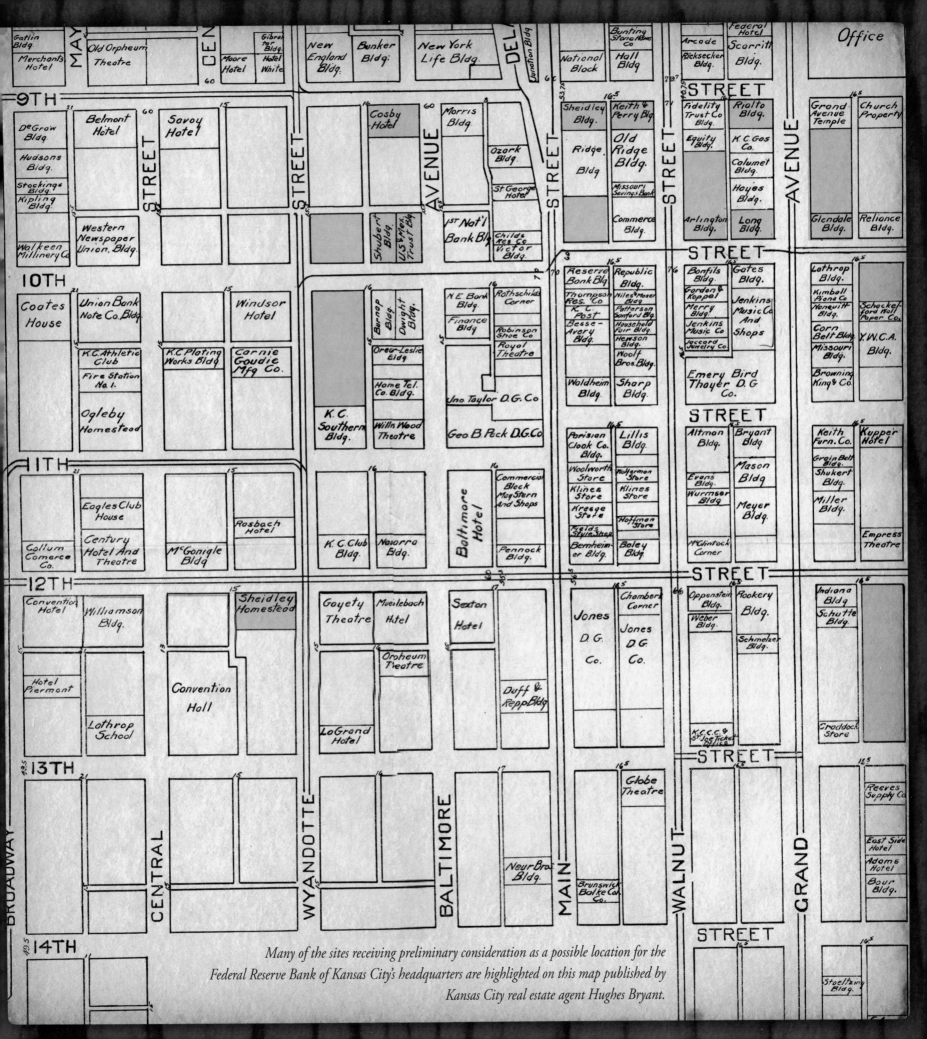

Many of the sites receiving preliminary consideration as a possible location for the Federal Reserve Bank of Kansas City's headquarters are highlighted on this map published by Kansas City real estate agent Hughes Bryant.

Location, location, location

After an initial consideration of at least 18 different locations in downtown Kansas City, the committee presented the Board of Directors with two reports on possible sites during a meeting on June 13, 1918:

- The northeast corner of 10th Street and Grand Avenue.[1] Ramsay and Gibson supported buying a tract of land measuring 144 feet by 115 feet if the Bank could negotiate a purchase price of $500,000.

- The southwest corner of Ninth Street and Baltimore Avenue. McClure favored buying a tract of land measuring 272 feet by 142 feet at a purchase price of $350,000.

The Glendale Building stood at the northeast corner of 10th Street and Grand Avenue in the years before the Federal Reserve Bank of Kansas City purchased the site as the location of its new headquarters.

1. Grand Avenue was renamed Grand Boulevard in 1993. It was given the honorary designation of Grand Boulevard of the Americas in 2007.

Although the Board supported a recommendation to purchase the Grand Avenue site, it was not a unanimous decision. Willis J. Bailey and C.E. Burnham joined McClure in voting against the recommendation.

Bailey elaborated his position in a letter he wrote two days later. Interestingly, Bailey opens the letter talking about building security – something that would be a key issue 85 years later when the Bank purchased 15 acres at 1 Memorial Drive to house a new headquarters.

"The (Ninth and Baltimore) location gives us ground space enough to place the building back from the streets and alleys and have a park around the entire building, separating the building from any other building, which, in my judgment, is a great advantage as a matter of security as well as giving the building the advantage of ventilation from every side."

Bailey goes on to note that the area was closer to hotels that could house visiting bankers and was cheaper than the site at 10th and Grand. The Baltimore site, he wrote, "will lend a dignity and personality to the building commensurate with the importance of the Federal Reserve Bank."

Although the letter was addressed to the Kansas City Bank, Worley's history suggests Bailey hoped his letter would prompt the Federal Reserve Board in Washington, D.C., to intervene and reverse the local Board's decision.[2] The Washington Board, however, refused to intervene and at a July 11 meeting the Kansas City Bank's Board of Directors voted to allow Bank Governor Miller to execute a contract on the site at 10th and Grand. The measure passed with Bailey and McClure voting against it.

Miller signed the contract the following day. According to a story in the July 12, 1918 edition of *The Kansas City Star*, the owners had originally asked $550,000, with the Bank agreeing to pay $500,000 for the property, which was then home to a two-story structure known as the Glendale Building, and a "bonus" of $25,000 to adjoining property owners.

Looking ahead toward construction, Kansas City newspapers suggested that the building would cost approximately $750,000 to construct. An article in *The Kansas City Journal* speculated it would contain a vault "several stories high. The vault, in fact, probably will be the same height as the building. Each vault floor will surpass anything in Kansas City."

2. The Bank forwarded Bailey's letter along with reports on both sites under consideration to the Federal Reserve Board. Bailey was also allowed to read his letter into the record at the Kansas City Board's July 11 meeting.

SITE HISTORY

925 Grand Boulevard

Before becoming home to the Federal Reserve Bank of Kansas City, the northeast corner of 10th and Grand had many owners in the city's early years.

According to documents in the Bank's archives and early newspaper accounts, the first owners of the property were Oliver Caldwell and Henry Childs, who purchased the tract from the government in 1834. A year

Around the turn of the century, the Grand Avenue Transfer Family Moving Co. operated out of a small building located near where the Federal Reserve Bank of Kansas City would later have its main entrance.

later, Childs sold his interest to Caldwell, who became one of the original incorporators of Kansas City in 1850. Caldwell, in turn, sold a 40-acre tract, including the future Bank site, to Thomas A. Smart for $400 on April 6, 1847. Smart held the property for about a decade, before selling it to Thomas A. Swope for $7,500 in the late 1850s.

Swope, who divided the land into lots creating "Swope's Addition," is well-known to Kansas Citians even today. Among his other projects, the developer and philanthropist most notably donated the land that became the city's most substantial public park: Swope Park, home to the city's zoo, Starlight Theater and other amenities.

Swope's parceling of the property along Grand divided the future Bank home into three separate lots that were bought and sold individually for nearly a half-century. At least two of the parcels became residences.

The first of the recorded homes was a three-room house on the middle of the three lots. It was likely built by George A. Torbet, who purchased the lot for $750 on April 6, 1869. The home was sold to Thomas J. Barnes for $1,300 on Oct. 23 of that year.

The corner lot contained a three-room house built by an unknown developer. Hiram and Mary Arbuckle lived in the home from 1877 until 1884, first renting the property for $15 a month and then later buying it for $1,100 from a Mr. Carswell who lived in Chicago. The home was the first known use of what would later become the Bank's address: 925 Grand.

Mary Arbuckle, who moved with her husband to Kansas City from Fort Scott, Kan., in the late 1870s, talked about the family's former home for a Jan. 6, 1922 story published by *The Kansas City Journal*:

"There were no houses on the hills to the west to obstruct our view, and we could see for many miles in several directions. Our home was 30 feet above Grand Avenue, and the street was reached by a wooden stairway from the front yard down to the ordinary level.

"An addition was built to the house which remained for many years until finally torn down to make way for other purposes. I remember well how people (could) stand in our yard and look over the surrounding country as we had a vantage point in several ways."

She recalled how, while living in the home, the couple predicted the property would be increasingly valuable in the years ahead.

The northeast corner of Grand Boulevard, then known as Grand Avenue, in 1894. A couple of residential roofs are visible at the top of the large clay hill. The Grand Avenue Methodist Church, which was razed for the construction of an office building in 1909, rises in the distance.

"Some day this property will be worth millions and our old home will be torn down," she told the *Journal* reporter. "I always could see a great future from the first time my husband and I came here in the early days."

The Arbuckles sold the property in 1884 for $8,000. The buyers are unknown.

The vacant lot

Although the Arbuckles might have seen a bright future for the property, it would be years before that vision was realized.

According to an item published in *The Kansas City Journal*, the former Arbuckle property, along with additional lots on what would become the Bank site, was purchased in early 1889 by the Amigo Realty and Investment Company for $60,000. Two months later, Amigo sold the property to George Smith Myers, a partner in Liggett & Myers Tobacco Company, for $79,200.

Myers apparently razed the houses on the property, but did little else.

The site became home to a massive mound of clay surrounded by billboards. On the Grand side of the property, at about the same location that would one day become the Bank's main entrance, stood the only known building - a small, shack-like structure that was the office for a company called Grand Avenue Transfer Family Moving Company.

Finally, in early 1910, Myers, who owned several downtown properties, announced plans to develop the site, eliminating what newspaper reports called one of the city's more prominent eyesores.

"That great hump of earth, which has long disfigured the lot at the northeast corner of Grand Avenue and 10th Street is rapidly giving way to an excavation for the basement of a new building," reads one newspaper account. "George S. Myers of St. Louis, who is erecting the structure, does not believe there is immediate need of another big office building and is erecting a temporary building of two stories and a basement of steel construction with brick and terra cotta facings."

The structure, called the Glendale Building after Myers' boyhood home near St. Louis, housed miscellaneous tenants, including offices for real estate companies and local political parties as well as a restaurant that was especially popular with Kansas City doctors and lawyers called the Tea Cup Inn.

Myers died not long after construction started on the building in 1910. In 1918, the Bank purchased the site for $500,000 from the Coppell, Cravens, Babcock Estate Company, heirs of the Myers estate.

GLENDALE MERCANTILE Co.

For a business that offered only a limited inventory to a select group of 300 customers, the Glendale Mercantile Co. received a lot of attention. And, for a brief period, it appeared poised to perhaps change the way groceries were sold throughout Kansas City.

The Glendale Mercantile Co. opened March 1, 1920, as a cooperative owned by employees of the Federal Reserve Bank of Kansas City. Portrayed in some newspaper articles as the brainchild of Bank Governor Jo Zach Miller, Jr., the store offered more than 100 non-perishable items for sale to cooperative members at prices that were essentially set at wholesale levels. The store's name was derived from the Glendale Building, a structure on the northeast corner of 10th Street and Grand Avenue that the Bank purchased as the eventual site of its new headquarters.

Almost 85 percent of the Bank's nearly 500 employees purchased $5 certificates to provide the store with capital.

The cooperative's operating procedures were described in a newspaper article published on its opening day:

"At 1 o'clock each day, a Bank employee will collect the orders, walk over to the Glendale Building and fill the orders ... (with) baskets or containers with the customers' name. At 4 o'clock, Bank office boys will carry the baskets to the Bank."

Despite making headlines locally, the Glendale Mercantile Co. was little more than a storage room filled with non-perishable items purchased by members of the cooperative.

The article said Miller was among the store's first customers, purchasing 17 items on the opening day.

The store was controversial from the start. Almost immediately after reports of its planned opening, the Retail Grocers' Association of Kansas City issued a bulletin to local wholesale distributors.

"We are all agreed that any plan for diverting business away from legitimately recognized channels of distribution is detrimental to the best interests of the grocery trade," the bulletin read.

Local wholesalers and packers, facing their own potential boycott by the city's grocers if they did business with the Bank, refused to sell goods to the Glendale Mercantile.

The cooperative, however, refused to buckle. According to an article later published by *The Kansas City Star*, the grocers' attempt to force the store out of business "aroused Mr. Miller's fighting spirit and he himself accepted the gauntlet."

Miller and other Bank officials defended the business to local reporters.

"We are simply doing a little welfare work for our business family, so that by taking home supplies in quantity they may do something to bring down, if possible, the high costs that the whole world is now attacking," Miller said in a newspaper inter-view. "We are not selling to the public, nor engaging in the grocery business for a profit. Elsewhere, large manufacturers and others including banks are conducting similar co-operative systems of selling food stuff."

The situation deteriorated. In another article, Assistant Bank Governor C.A. Worthington suggested the cooperative might open its doors to the public.

"(The grocers) have demanded that the wholesalers refuse to sell us goods if we limit our sales to Bank employees," Worthington said. "They say that we should not be sold any supplies unless we sell them to the public at large. And if the situation continues, that is just what we may do and we will sell staple groceries at wholesale prices to whoever wants to buy."

The Kansas City Post published an editorial supporting the store and suggesting it should, in fact, be opened to the general public. The paper went so far as to volunteer to "throw open its front page to tell the public how money can be saved by patronizing the store."

"The effort of the employees of the Federal Reserve Bank to lower the cost of living by combining and buying their groceries at wholesale prices is an experiment that should have the hearty support of everyone," the *Post* editorial said.

Another newspaper article said other Kansas City-area businesses were closely watching the Bank's store and considering similar ventures of their own. Among them, one unnamed major firm with some 3,000 workers.

Eventually, the embargo was broken and the store continued to operate, moving to the R.A. Long Building when the Glendale Building was demolished to make way for the new Bank headquarters. It later moved into the new Bank in November 1921, operating out of space on the building's fourth floor until it closed in 1922.

The then-upcoming closing was announced in an Aug. 6, 1922 article in *The Kansas City Star*.

"The least conspicuous grocery in Kansas City, a spic and span little shop tucked away on the fourth floor of the Federal Reserve Bank, is fading toward a total eclipse," *The Star* wrote. "The big Bank will close out the little cooperative shop Aug. 15."

According to the article, Bank officials said the fact that the closing came less than two months after Miller's departure from the Bank was merely coincidental.

"Gov. Miller, shortly before his departure, conceded the grocery had outlived its usefulness and raised the question of discontinuing the store," Asa Ramsay, chairman of the Bank's Board of Directors, told *The Star*. "With lower living costs, such an emergency has passed."

The unrealistically massive vault imagined by the writer suggests the level of excitement about the project and what it signified for both the Bank and the city. The same sentiment was reflected in the article's opening paragraph:

"The new Federal Reserve Bank building…will be more truly the financial Heart of the Southwest than anyone imagined…"

"The new Federal Reserve Bank building the directors of this district have recommended be placed at the northeast corner of 10th Street and Grand Avenue will be more truly the financial heart of the Southwest than anyone imagined when the regional bank was won for Kansas City in 1914."

Bank officials hoped for rapid construction and a quick move into the new headquarters.

"Need for a new quarters is urgent," Miller told a *Kansas City Journal* reporter in November 1918. "We hope that by starting to work immediately the building will be ready for occupancy in a year and a half."

As it turned out, it would be another 18 months after Miller's comment before construction could even start.

THE DESIGN

Perhaps in hopes of speeding the design process, the Bank's directors produced a fairly extensive list of design requirements to provide to any architects interested in the project. Among other provisions, there were specifics about the building's height, that it would need two-story high granite columns along Grand Avenue, and that it must house an ornate and impressive lobby.

Their focus on the design detail, however, may have left them vulnerable to another issue.

When word spread that the Bank was considering a Chicago firm, and not one of the seven Kansas City firms that were seeking the job, a group of local business leaders, including well-known developer J.C. Nichols, demanded a meeting with the Bank's building committee. When the Nov. 22, 1918 meeting ended, the Bank announced the selection process would be delayed for at least a day.

"It is purely a business proposition and I am sure that Mr. Miller and his colleagues are as anxious as any citizens to see the interests of the city protected," Nichols told a reporter. "But we have the best architects in the country in Kansas City."

Less than a week later, the Bank's Board selected the Chicago architectural firm Graham, Anderson, Probst and White for the project.

In local newspaper accounts, Miller attempted to soothe his critics, saying the Bank would consider local contractors and materials dealers first as the project advanced.

The comments did little to calm at least one local resident who fired off an angry and anonymous letter to the editor ridiculing everything from Miller's unique first name to his promise of considering Kansas City construction firms.

"It was shabby, cheap and humiliating to sweep Kansas City architects aside when a Kansas City building was to be erected," the critic wrote. He concluded the letter saying he hoped "the new building looks like a brick oven."

The proposed height of the Federal Reserve Bank of Kansas City's headquarters changed several times during the planning process. This early rendering of an 11-story structure is very similar to the resulting 21-story building.

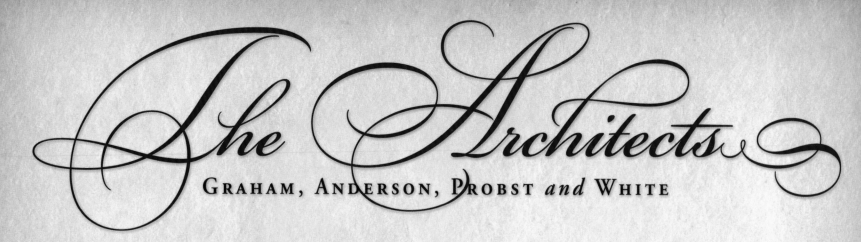

The Architects

GRAHAM, ANDERSON, PROBST and WHITE

The architectural firm that designed the Federal Reserve Bank of Kansas City's headquarters at 10th Street and Grand was a successor to one of the most important firms in U.S. architectural history.

Graham, Anderson, Probst and White traced its history to the partnership of Burnham and Root - pioneers in the Chicago school of architecture and modern skyscraper design. Their work included several late-1800s skyscrapers that still stand today in Chicago, including the Monadnock Building and the Rookery, both historically significant buildings. The firm designed seven buildings in Kansas City, including the city's second Board of Trade building, which stood at 210 W. Eighth St. from 1888 to 1968.

The firm became D.H. Burnham and Company after Root's death of pneumonia in 1891, and was notable for, among other things, Burnham's work as chief architect of Chicago's 1893 World's Columbian Exposition and the design of the Flatiron Building in New York City, considered by some to be that city's oldest skyscraper.

After Burnham's death in 1912, Burnham's sons, Daniel Jr. and Hubert, joined long-time apprentices Ernest Graham, Pierce Anderson, Edward Probst and Howard White to form Graham, Burnham and Company. The groups split in 1917, with the sons going into business as D.H. Burnham and Company and the four former apprentices opening Graham, Anderson, Probst and White.

The firm's design for the Federal Reserve Bank of Kansas City's headquarters is described in great detail over several pages of the Bank's 1920 annual report.

According to the report, the overall design was expected to produce "an effect of simplicity and dignity.

"The general effect of the entire exterior will be that of a field of windows grouped two-by-two, surrounded by a heavy stone frame and tied together across the top by a sloping pediment, forming an effect of strength and solidity."

The report also describes the building's interior, including the lobby. With its towering pillars, the room is designed to resemble the colonnaded hall of the Temple of Karnak in Egypt, of which Bank Governor Jo Zach Miller, Jr., was reportedly fond.

Although visitors would sometimes note how much the lobby of the Federal Reserve Bank building at 925 Grand clearly identifies the building as a central bank, the architects who designed it drew inspiration from the Temple of Karnak in Egypt.

"The principal aim in (the lobby's) design was not the creation of an overpowering architectural effect, but rather the achievement of a banking room which would be open, spacious and well-lighted," reads the annual report.

Interestingly, the annual report also makes reference to a rooftop "playground" which would be accessible through a gymnasium also on the building's top floor. The playground was not built.

In addition to the Federal Reserve Bank of Kansas City building, Graham, Anderson, Probst and White designed the Federal Reserve Bank of Chicago's headquarters and other Chicago landmarks including the Wrigley Building, Field Museum of Natural History and Shedd Aquarium.

The Temple of
KARNAK

HIGHER *and* HIGHER

While the selection of an out-of-town architect may have caused a delay of a few days, the problem was minimal compared with the time lost as Bank officials wrestled with the question of the building's height.

From the start, there was not agreement on how many stories the Bank needed. Prior to choosing an architect, documents in the Bank archives indicate that Miller favored a 21-story building, a giant in a city where two, 16-story buildings had towered above the skyline for more than a dozen years. Miller's vision was also a skyscraper compared with the thoughts of the building committee – at least one committee member felt as few as six floors would suffice, while others preferred a building between eight and 12 stories.

> *"This building has been very close to my heart because we are building a* Great Instrument *of service for this territory…"*

The building committee eventually decided on an eight-story structure, but changed that requirement days later, saying the building needed to be 10 stories. In February 1919, Kansas City newspapers published a design rendering of an 11-story structure. A month later it was announced that the structure would be built with a foundation capable of eventually supporting a 21-story building and that the Bank hoped to start construction in July.

The plans were revised during the summer and by August, a month after the planned start of construction, the Bank announced it would build a 16-story structure when work began.

"That a 10-story building soon would have been cramped is indicated by the fact that the Reserve Bank is planning to devote 10 floors of the new structure to its own purposes," *The Kansas City Star* wrote in the Aug. 9, 1919 edition. "Of the remaining six floors, three probably will be used by various government offices while three floors will be leased commercially."

The change to 16 stories added about 60 days to the planning process. Bank officials said, under the revised timeline, they expected to begin razing the Glendale Building, which stood on the site, by Oct. 1 and begin construction two weeks later.

The Builder
George A. Fuller Company

he contractor that built the Federal Reserve Bank of Kansas City's headquarters was one of the most prominent builders of early U.S. skyscrapers.

The George A. Fuller Company was the builder of many of the early skyscrapers designed by the legendary architectural firm of Burnham and Root, including the Monadnock Building and the Rookery in Chicago, as well as Burnham's Flatiron Building in New York City, which was briefly known as the Fuller Building while the company was headquartered there. Among its numerous other projects were the construction of the Lincoln Memorial and the U.S. Supreme Court building, both in Washington, D.C.

Before it was selected to build the Federal Reserve Bank of Kansas City in 1920, the company had already completed several projects in Kansas City, including Union Station and, soon after, Children's Mercy Hospital. Today, both buildings are near the Bank's new headquarters at 1 Memorial Drive.

The firm was in business until the 1970s when it was sold.

Kansas City's Union Station was one of several projects built by the George A. Fuller Co., builder of the Federal Reserve Bank of Kansas City's headquarters at 925 Grand.

10-1-12

It did not happen, and in December 1919, the Federal Reserve Board put all Federal Reserve Bank construction projects on hold.

"A careful survey of building conditions has demonstrated the fact that building materials and construction costs recently have advanced to too high a point to justify the Board in authorizing building at this time," *The Kansas City Times* reported in its Dec. 12, 1919 edition.

The regional Reserve Banks were instructed to spend the following months finalizing their building plans. The Bank apparently expected a delay of two or three months, telling Glendale Building tenants they could remain in that facility until March 1, 1920.

Finally, nearly two years after the Bank had purchased the property, it was able to move forward with the project, awarding a contract to build a 305-foot building, or 21 stories, to the George A. Fuller Company, builders of Kansas City's Union Station, on April 16, 1920. Coincidentally, the deal with Fuller came on Miller's 57th birthday.

Kansas City's Grand Avenue was home to the city's skyscrapers in the early years of the 20th century. One of the buildings in the background of this postcard is the R.A. Long Building, one of Kansas City's two tallest buildings at the time and then home to the Federal Reserve Bank of Kansas City, which was preparing to build its own high rise across the street.

Grand Ave. South from 8th
Kansas City, Mo.

"This is the most satisfactory birthday of my life," Miller said in a story published the following day in *The Kansas City Star.* "It is more than a recognition of Kansas City's position in finance in the Southwest. That we are able to do this is justification of the wisdom shown originally in placing one of the Federal (Reserve) Banks in this city. But this building has been very close to my heart because we are building a great instrument of service for this territory, and every bit of efficiency the Bank gains is a contribution toward the welfare of a section of the country to which, I trust, we are all devoted. We are building on a large scale, but the future will show that we have not been over-optimistic."

Opposition

Although newspaper accounts suggest a drawn-out process led Bank officials from eight to 21 stories, Bank officials had apparently decided early on – perhaps more than a full year before signing the contract with Fuller – that their preference was for a 21-story structure that would include room for future growth. They were unwilling to move forward with that plan, however, in the face of resistance from downtown neighbors who opposed what would be the city's tallest structure.

Documents in the Bank's archives indicate that the formal complaints started in March 1919, around the time the Bank publicly announced plans for an 11-story building with a base capable of one day supporting a full 21 stories.

The objections, however, were never aired publicly. A *Kansas City Journal* article published on April 11, 1919, said problems getting the project started were the result of "Washington red tape alone."

"No evidence of a sentiment for holding down Kansas City's skyline seems to have crystallized, in fact owners of skyscrapers that would be dwarfed by the proposed 21-story federal structure generally favor 'no limit' and no forced uniformity for Kansas City," the newspaper wrote.

Actually, the primary critics were the owners of the city's other large office buildings. The Commerce Trust Company Building and the R.A. Long Building, considered the city's first skyscrapers when they were built in 1906, were both located near the Bank's site. The owners apparently feared the buildings would be overshadowed by a Bank building some five stories higher.

R.A. Long was one of the Kansas City area's most prominent residents in the early 20th century. Long's country estate was Longview Farm. His family donated the land that became Longview Community College and they sold other properties that modern-day Kansas Citians know as Longview Lake.

At a March 25, 1919 meeting, the directors of the National Bank of Commerce passed a formal resolution condemning the idea of a 21-story Federal Reserve building and calling for a meeting with local Federal Reserve officials.

"Technically, the objection was based on the assumption that the city's skyline would appear uneven and that other companies or corporations expecting to build buildings in the future might again outstrip the new (Federal Reserve) building and thus in a manner belittle the two ranking business buildings who had pioneered the tall building," reads the account in Worley's Bank history.

The Commerce group that met with Bank officials included two men who had unique connections with the Federal Reserve Bank of Kansas City:

- Commerce Chairman William T. Kemper originally brought Bank Gov. Miller to Kansas City in 1910 to work at Commerce and supported his selection to head the Federal Reserve Bank of Kansas City. Commerce would also later employ members of the Miller family for the next two generations.

- R.A. Long was the owner of the R.A. Long Building where the Bank had leased space to serve as its headquarters since its opening in 1914. Later, after Miller retired from the Bank, he worked on a bondholders committee trying to save Long's Long-Bell Lumber Company.

The third member of the Commerce committee was the developer Nichols, who had previously met with Bank officials as a leading critic of the architect selection process.

Bank officials at the meeting were Ramsay, McClure and Miller.

Nichols spoke on the Commerce group's behalf, explaining their position and then suggesting the Bank purchase additional property to house a wider, shorter building.

"In answer it was pointed out to the objectors that when the Long Building was erected, it far outstripped the surrounding skyline and no objection was raised, also that the operations of the Bank required the maximum of natural light and fresh air and that the height of the building was intended to take care of these requirements as well as to utilize the very high-priced ground to the best advantage," Worley writes.

The disagreement delayed the project.

According to Worley, "the Federal Reserve Bank directors did not desire to make the request of the Federal Reserve Board for the (full) 21-story building while there were extant any objections on the part of any Kansas City businessmen."

There is no record of how the two sides were able to resolve their issues, although, according to Worley, Commerce directors eventually informed the Federal Reserve that their resolution of objection had been expunged from their records. By that time, Worley writes, the project had been

Legendary Kansas City developer J.C. Nichols was critical of the Federal Reserve Bank of Kansas City's building project. After arguing against the use of an out-of-town architect, he later tried to convince Bank officials to purchase more property and build a wider, shorter building instead of a 21-story structure.

delayed by several months. Another account in the Bank archives suggests the objection ended up adding as much as a full year to the process – a delay that, by some estimates, ended up increasing the Bank's project cost by at least $500,000.

But finally, in the spring of 1920, work was ready to begin.

Demolition of the Glendale Building started May 13 and was concluded at midnight on June 4. Excavation for the new building began three days later.

Demolition of the Glendale Building moved quickly. The building was stripped to its key supports four days after workers began razing the structure.

GLENDALE BUILDING BEING DEMOLISHED.
MAY 17, 1920.

TRAGEDY *and* DELAY

As with any large-scale construction project in the era before modern safety regulations, work on the Federal Reserve Bank of Kansas City had its share of tragedies, the first coming early in the project.

On Aug. 7, 1920, a Kansas City woman was hit by flying stones when a metal covering, designed to catch debris from blasts creating the pit for the building's foundation, failed. Hazel Teachenor, 30, was on her way home from her job in a downtown office building and was on the southwest corner of 10th and Grand when she was struck in the head by the 2-inch stone, fracturing her skull. Although the first media accounts of the event suggested the injuries would likely prove fatal, Teachenor survived. According to an unpublished *Kansas City Star* article written sometime in late 1921 and filed in *The Star's* archives, Teachenor's "life was saved only after an extremely delicate operation."

It is perhaps a miracle that more people were not hurt in the incident. According to newspaper accounts, although the blasts were set off more than 40 feet below street level, they sent a barrage of stones into a street crowded with hundreds of people on their way home. [3]

With Kansas Citians regularly crowding nearby sidewalks to watch construction of the city's new skyscraper, it may be surprising to learn that Teachenor was the only citizen injured during the project. Luck was certainly on the side of construction watchers late in the project when the boom of a hoisting derrick on top of the building broke, sending a 600-pound stone hurtling to the street more than 20 stories below.

"Although Grand Avenue was teeming with its morning rush of passing pedestrians and motor cars, no one was injured…"

"Although Grand Avenue was teeming with its morning rush of passing pedestrians and motor cars, no one was injured by the flying fragments of stone sent in all directions when the ornamental buttress plunged … (and) tore a huge hole in the asphalt pavement just east of the street railway tracks," *The Kansas City Journal* reported in its July 20, 1921 edition.

Workers on the roof were not as lucky. Edward Hager, a stonesetter's assistant, had his right arm and leg severed by the swinging boom and died of his injuries within minutes. Two other workers

3. The incident also touched off a brief debate about construction blasting within the city limits.

Reward Offered

In the early years of the 20th century, easterners may have still considered much of the Tenth Federal Reserve District to be the "Wild West." Unfortunately, some in the District were doing little to overcome that perception.

Documents associated with 1920 federal legislation to increase the penalties for bank robbery specifically noted a high number of incidents in the Tenth Federal Reserve District.

"I wish to say that the attention of the (Federal Reserve) Board has been called to frequent holdups and robberies from which banks have suffered, principally in the Kansas City Federal Reserve district," Federal Reserve Governor W.P.G. Harding wrote in a letter to Sen. Knute Nelson, chair of the Senate Judiciary Committee.

In an attempt to counter the problem, the Federal Reserve Bank of Kansas City planned to take the unusual step of offering rewards for tips leading authorities to bank robbers.

Harding's letter to Nelson included a circular the Kansas City Bank hoped to distribute:

"One thousand dollars reward is offered by the Federal Reserve Bank of Kansas City for the arrest and conviction of any person or persons found guilty of burglarizing or robbing, after this date, by force of arms, any bank or trust company, member or nonmember of the Federal Reserve System, within the Tenth District, of securities of the United States issued since April 1917."

The circular, which was to be sent out under the signature of Bank Governor Jo Zach Miller, Jr., goes on to state specific requirements related to how the reward will be distributed.

Harding's letter to Nelson, dated Nov. 4, 1919, indicates the Federal Reserve's legal counsel determined the System did not have the legal authority to justify offering a reward. The circular was never distributed.

ONE KILLED AS HOIST SNAPS ON FEDERAL BANK ROOF

E. D. Hager Dies and Two Others Injured When 600-Pound Stone Falls 18 Stories to Street.

TRAM CAR JUST OUT OF ROCK'S PATH

Lives of Many Pedestrians and Autoists Are Periled by Fall of Huge Granite Block.

One man was killed almost instantly and two others were injured, shortly before 10 o'clock Tuesday morning, when the boom of a hoisting derrick broke on the roof of the new Federal Reserve Bank building, Tenth street and Grand avenue.

were injured in the incident blamed on faulty equipment.

Hager's death came three months after the project's only other known fatality. On April 15, 1921, engineer John Rogers died from injuries he suffered after being struck in the head. Rogers was working in the building's basement when a plumber's helper on the 14th floor lost his balance and fell to the building's 13th floor, dropping a metal cap he had been placing on a 5-inch pipe. The cap pierced an inch-thick board before hitting Rogers.

The project also had two labor-related issues.

Work was halted for three days after 55 workers walked off the job in protest of the firing of a union carpenter in August 1920. A planned strike was avoided in the spring of 1921 after carpenters and sheet metal workers were able to resolve an issue regarding responsibility for installing metal window casings and doors. The threatened strike would have involved carpenters' union workers on Fuller projects in Kansas City, Chicago, New York and Tulsa. In Kansas City, as the threatened strike deadline drew near, the Building Trades Council sought and received a restraining order that would have forced the carpenters to continue working on the Federal Reserve project. The Kansas City Building Trades Council also sent a contingent to Indianapolis to work on a settlement between the two unions.

Construction

Begins

Excavation work at 925 Grand started on June 7, 1914, with construction following soon after. The site offices of builder George A. Fuller Company are clearly visible near the top of the photo. Following pages: A series of photos show the rise of what would be Kansas City's tallest building at the time of its completion.

No. 21 Taken SEPT. 23, 1920
FEDERAL RESERVE BANK Building
KANSAS City
GRAHAM ANDERSON Probst White Architect
GEORGE A. FULLER Co. BUILDERS

THE SCULPTOR and THE COIN

The two sculpted stone panels adorning the front of the Federal Reserve Bank building at 925 Grand Boulevard were prepared by a man whose work was at one time featured by nearly half the nation's regional Reserve Banks and who was involved in the creation of the gold coin that many consider the most beautiful in U.S. history.

Henry Hering's work "covered a broad field from medals and portrait medallions to monumental works," *The New York Times* wrote in his 1949 obituary.

For the Federal Reserve Bank of Kansas City, Hering created the Sprit of Industry and the Spirit of Commerce, both two stories high and rising above Grand Boulevard near the Bank's main entrance.

A published item about the sculptures explained their design:

"As the Federal Reserve banking system promotes and stabilizes industry and commerce, not only in the United States but over the whole world, the symbolical figures of Industry and Commerce are represented as standing on a cloud-surrounded globe, supported by an eagle on the breast of which is shown the seal of the Federal Reserve Bank."

Industry, which is the northern sculpture, holds a sheaf of wheat and a distaff, representing agriculture and manufacturing. A bee hive appears above her head. Commerce, meanwhile, wears a coat of mail to signify security and holds a torch of progress. The ship of Transportation

A drawing depicting Henry Hering taking matters into his own hands on the Spirit of Industry on the front of the Federal Reserve Bank of Kansas City. Among his numerous accomplishments, the sculptor also played an important role in the 1907 redesign of the $20 Double Eagle gold coin.

floats above her head.

Hering, who was paid $5,000 for his work, offered the Bank two choices. A second option featured essentially the same figures, but instead of the items signifying commerce and industry, one held a banner reading "Integrity" and the other a banner reading "Security."

The sculptor produced models for each of the panels, but made at least one trip to Kansas City to inspect the full-size pieces. According to a newspaper account, Hering was not entirely satisfied with the work and climbed onto the scaffolding, took a mallet and chisel from one of the workers "and proceeded to deepen a shadow here and there."

Although the carving of the actual sculptures was based on "a thousand small measurements by skilled artisans," *The New York Times* said "they are seldom skilled enough for this sculptor."

In addition to the pieces for the Federal Reserve Bank of Kansas City, Hering also did contract work for the Federal Reserve Banks in Chicago, Cleveland and Dallas. He did architectural work for several buildings including Chicago's Field Museum of Natural History.

On a different scale, Hering was also involved in the 1907 redesign of the $20 Double Eagle gold coin.

President Theodore Roosevelt asked Hering's mentor, legendary American sculptor Augustus Saint-Gaudens, to redesign the coin into something similar to those used in ancient Greece. After completing the design, however, Saint-Gaudens health began to decline and he turned the project over to Hering, who was then his assistant.

Hering engaged in a lengthy battle with Charles Barber, the Mint's chief engraver. Saint-Gaudens' design required as many as 11 strikes from the Mint's press to produce the high level of detail in the artwork. Barber, likely already angry that the Mint had been asked to produce a coin designed by an outside artist for the first time, argued that the production process was impractical.

Saint-Gaudens did not live to see the dispute resolved. He died three months before the Mint, under direct order from Roosevelt, finally began production of the coins.

Relatively few of the coins were produced in the high relief sought by Hering and his mentor. Commercial banks complained that the coins, which also were costly for the Mint to manufacture, would not lie flat and did not stack easily.

It was not the only criticism of the design.

Early editions displayed the date in Roman numerals instead of the traditional Arabic numerals. The early coins also did not include the words "In God We Trust," which, although not required, had become common.

Changes were soon made and later editions were produced using Arabic numerals and in a standard relief. In response to the public outcry, Congress in 1908 also passed legislation requiring "In God We Trust" to

Hering's Spirit of Industry (left) and Spirit of Commerce were created to adorn the front of the Bank. Today, statues based on the two Hering pieces stand in front of the Bank's headquarters at 1 Memorial Drive.

appear on all U.S. coins.

Visitors to the Federal Reserve Bank of Kansas City can see early and later versions of the Double Eagle coins in the Harry S. Truman coin collection on display in the Bank's lobby. The 1907 coin is notably thicker and of significantly higher detail than those produced in the following years. It also features the Roman numerals – a sign that it was among the first coins produced. Those looking at the display will also notice the unique placement of the words "E Pluribus Unum," which appear along the edge of the coin.

In addition to his sculptures and his work on the Double Eagle coin, Hering was briefly in the public spotlight as one of the victims of one of the more bizarre and tragic events in New York City history. When a B-25 bomber, lost in dense fog, crashed into the Empire State Building in July 1945, debris rained down upon Hering's penthouse studio in a neighboring building.

The artist was out of town golfing at the time of the accident and returned to find $75,000 in damage. Among the notable works destroyed in the incident was a 22-foot-tall model of "Pro Patria," used by Hering to create the central figure in Indiana's War Memorial, that was valued at $10,000.

He died on Jan. 17, 1949.

Ceremony

Construction on the building moved quickly. The first steel column was placed on Jan. 5, 1921, and three months later, the last was attached. At a "topping out" ceremony on April 9, 1921, workers and Bank officials raised a flag on the building's southwest corner to signify that the structure had reached its final height.

According to an account in *The Kansas City Star*, those participating in the ceremony had to "toil … up steps and ladders for 19 floors" to reach the event.

Federal Reserve Bank of Kansas City Gov. Jo Zach Miller, Jr. (front, center) and other Bank officials join workers from the George A. Fuller Company in hoisting a flag atop the Bank's new headquarters during a "topping out" ceremony on April 9, 1921.

"The little group stood higher than any banker had ever been before in Kansas City," *The Star* reporter wrote in an account that also noted the temperature was five degrees cooler at the top of the structure than at street level.

Ramsay, the chair of the Bank's Board of Directors, made brief comments during the ceremony, referencing the climb to the top of the building and mentioning the nation's most well-known elevator manufacturer.

"Mr. Otis is a great man, probably the world's greatest benefactor," Ramsay said, according to *The Star's* account.

A week later, at noon on Saturday, April 16, 1921, the Bank hosted the far more formal and elaborate cornerstone ceremony on an especially unseasonable day that *The Kansas City Post* described as "a blinding snowstorm."[4]

Still, an estimated 500 people attended the event, including the governors of the District's seven states as well as 13 U.S. senators, 32 members of the U.S. House of Representatives, state bank commissioners and banking association heads from each District state, numerous bankers and Kansas City dignitaries, and even the presidents of the region's major universities.

Highlights of the day included speeches from Miller and Bank Directors Ramsay and Bailey as well as the singing of "To Thee, O Country" and "Stars and Stripes Forever" by the Federal Reserve Choral Club.

"As the strains of music floated down over Grand Avenue … hundreds of pedestrians paused to listen," *The Post* reporter wrote. "Their eyes lifted upward in awe to the towering … building being dedicated. The streets remained lined with spectators throughout the ceremonies."

The cornerstone was inscribed with the letters A.M.D.G. for "Ad Majorem Die Glorium," meaning "To the Greater Glory of God." The letters appear above the words "Industry – Agriculture – Commerce," which were explained by Ramsay during his remarks as "signifying that industry is the foundation of

Federal Reserve Bank of Kansas City Gov. Jo Zach Miller, Jr., during the cornerstone ceremony at the Bank's headquarters building, April 16, 1921.

4. Construction, however, benefited from periods of mild weather during the winter months and unusually mild conditions in early March.

THE FBI

The Federal Reserve is sometimes referred to as "the Fed." However, actual "Feds," as in federal law enforcement agents, were office tenants in the Bank building during the investigation of one of the most infamous crimes in Kansas City history.

Then known as the Bureau of Investigation, and briefly as the Division of Investigation, the FBI had offices on the west side of the Bank's ninth floor from 1928 through late 1933. After relocating for six months, the FBI returned to the Bank in 1934 with larger offices on the 16th floor. It was a period of time when the agency rapidly was evolving into what it is today.

Everything changed on June 17, 1933.

Union Station Massacre

The story of the Union Station Massacre is well-known in Kansas City history.

According to the official FBI report, gangster Charles "Pretty Boy" Floyd and accomplices Vernon Miller and Adam Richetti attempted to free Frank Nash, a prisoner being transported back to the U.S. penitentiary at Leavenworth, Kan. Nash had escaped three years earlier and was recaptured in Hot Springs, Ark., by federal agents Frank Smith and Joe Lackey.

The two agents, and Otto Reed, the chief of police in McAlester, Okla., escorted Nash out of the train station to the car of agent Raymond Caffrey, who was joined by Reed Vetterli, special agent in charge of the Bureau's Kansas City office, and Kansas City Police Detectives W.J. Grooms and Frank Hermanson. According to FBI records, Floyd, Miller and Richetti came forward as the men were getting into the car, with one yelling, "Let 'em have it."

The event was reported in that evening's edition of *The Kansas City Star*:

"Kansas City's Union Station plaza became an arena of horror at 7:20 o'clock this morning when eight men were ambushed with machine guns, five of them killed outright, and a sixth critically wounded in a brief but murderous burst of fire."

Vetterli, who was shot in the left arm during the exchange, described the scene in an Associated Press story:

"Caffrey stood on the pavement beside (the prisoner) Nash on the east side of the car waiting for Nash to slide over into the folding front seat. Hermanson and Grooms were standing on the west side of the car and toward the front. Suddenly, I heard a man say, 'Put 'em up, up, up.'

"I looked and saw a man blazing away with a machine gun from near the southwest corner of the car. He seemed to be standing on something – perhaps the running board of a car, I don't know exactly, but was very close to us.

One of the memos by Bank Building Superintendent D.A. Lilla which led to FBI agents being able to utilize the firing range that had been built for use by the Bank's own security staff.

M E M O R A N D

July 3, 193

Mr. Helm:

Mr. R. E. Vetterli, Spe
Bureau of Investigation, Rooms 9
has made a verbal request to the
if consistent with the policy of
special agents to use our target
for revolver target practice.

In view of the above sp
gaged in special and confidentia
tions and probably less than one
the use of the range periodicall,
your advising us as to your deci
as soon as possible in order tha
Vetterli.

FEDERAL

By

DAL:LT

"I crouched under the murderous fire. I believe there were other machine guns working, too."

The moments after the shooting are detailed in the 2004 book "Public Enemies: America's Greatest Crime Wave and the Birth of the FBI, 1933-34," by Bryan Burrough:

"Vetterli, bleeding lightly from his arm wound, rushed to the FBI offices in the Federal Reserve Bank building. He picked up the phone, called Washington, and was put through to the director.

"'It was a massacre, Mr. Hoover,' Vetterli said."

Killed in the incident were Caffrey, Grooms, Hermanson and Reed. It was the second-largest murder of law enforcement officers in American history at that time.

Lackey and Vetterli were injured. The attempt to free Nash was unsuccessful – he also was killed in the shootout.

Although Vetterli and others returned fire, the attackers escaped. Floyd, Miller and Richetti all later denied involvement in the incident. Six months after the attack, Miller was killed by Detroit mobsters. In October 1934, Floyd was killed in a shootout with FBI agents on an Ohio farm. Richetti was arrested in 1934 and later executed in the Missouri penitentiary's gas chamber.

The aftermath

The attack changed the FBI. At the time, agents did not have the authority to regularly carry firearms or make arrests. That authority was granted among a series of changes in the months that followed.

Two weeks after the attack, a memo from the Bank building's superintendent to the head of the Bank's security cleared the way for FBI agents to begin using a firing range that had been created for use by the Bank's own security staff.

"Please understand that the use of our range by the agents mentioned above and under the supervision of Mr. Vetterli is confidential in all respects," a July 1933 memo from Building Superintendent D.A. Lilla concludes.

It is quite possible the Federal Reserve's security staff, which was accustomed to carrying weapons, assisted local FBI agents with their training. The FBI's unfamiliarity with guns is noted in Robert Unger's 1997 book "The Union Station Massacre," where Unger quotes from a 1983 interview he conducted with Agent Ray C. Suran.

"We had one, thirty-two caliber pistol in the Kansas City office. That was it," Suran told Unger. "I was told one time to get the gun and some bullets and come to a particular office. When I got there, I found out the bullets wouldn't even fit the gun. They were the wrong caliber."

Although the FBI moved out of the Bank building and into another nearby location in September 1933, FBI agents were still allowed access to the Bank's firing range, according to a handwritten note on the July 1933 memo.

The FBI was not away long, returning to the Bank building in June 1934, with offices in the northeast corner of the 16th floor. The agency's new powers are evident in correspondence with Building Superintendent Lilla. While the previous lease had required only office space, the FBI required the construction of a holding cell in its second lease with the Bank. Cell specifications were detailed in a Feb. 5, 1935 memo:

"Walls of cage to be constructed of vertical 7/8 inch diameter round bars made of cold rolled steel spaced 4-inch center to center properly braced. Top to be of bullet-proof spring steel mesh wire 10 gauge-inch mesh."

The Bank estimated it would cost $302.75 to build the cell, which was later constructed in the extreme northeast corner of the 16th floor.

In a 1996 interview, one of the Bank's elevator operators in the 1930s, Sam Pauly, described the holding cell as a "vault" that measured 12 feet by 14 feet. He recalled seeing the federal officers bringing apparent suspects into the building bound with chains around their legs and wrists.

The FBI moved out of the Bank building in 1939.

all our happiness and achievements; that without industry there would be no agriculture and without agriculture there would be no commerce."

Ramsay also noted the contents of a time capsule sealed inside the stone, including a piece from an old prairie schooner built near Kansas City before the Civil War, as well as items from each state in the District, including wheat and corn from the District's farmland, a lump of coal from New Mexico, mineral deposits from Colorado, and numerous other tokens and items.

The chairman of the Bank's Board of Directors then introduced Miller.

"More than three years ago Gov. Miller first suggested the idea of such a structure as this. With a remarkable foresight and vision, which has characterized all his undertakings, Gov. Miller declared over the protest and embarrassing opposition of many who honestly differed with him, that the building should be high enough to take care of the expansion of the Bank," Ramsay said. "Is there anyone here who has watched the development of this great institution as one function after another has been added to it and observed the various departments crowd each other in their growth who would consent that one story should be removed? It has been a great achievement and a laborious task of love for him."

A piece of a prairie schooner built near Kansas City was modified to include some vials of various items from the Tenth Federal Reserve District and placed inside the cornerstone of the Bank's building at 925 Grand.

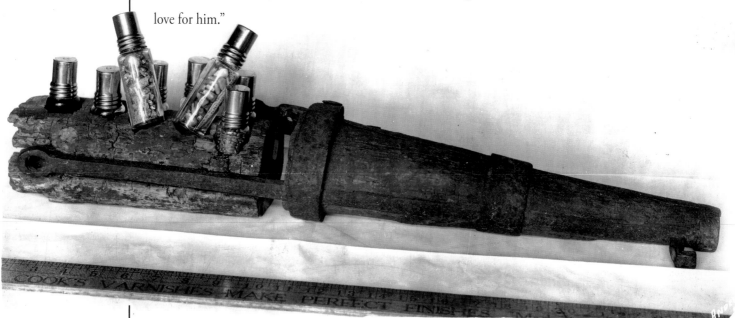

Miller, who marked his 58th birthday on the day of the ceremony, placed the stone using a gold trowel with an ivory handle. The Bank's directors later presented Miller with the trowel, which is now on display in the current Bank headquarters.

"This Bank building, standing within a stone's throw of the ravine that once marked the Santa Fe Trail, belongs to and typifies the great Southwestern territory which was once threaded by this great trail and its branches," Miller said in his remarks. "Those trails were the arteries and veins that fed this infant empire and made it fit for the great country it is today; that made this Bank and banking system not only possible but necessary. The success and future of this institution will be the success and future of the Tenth Federal Reserve District."

"The Success and Future of this institution will be the success and future of the Tenth Federal Reserve District."

The placement was described in *The Post*:

"The cornerstone ceremony was brief. Gov. Miller quickly lifted a trowel of mortar and performed the first act that will forever fix the stone in its place to dedicate to future generations the use of the building."

The writer, who noted that by the end of the event many guests were covered with snow, also described the scene at the time the stone was placed:

"Every seat under the tented shelter was occupied by guests of the Bank. Many others stood about on the platform, forgetting the chill wind that whipped about the steel work of the structure. Hundreds of spectators crowded about the base of the building on 10th Street and Grand Avenue, and others took vantage points on the farther corners from the building."

Cornerstone ceremony

Truman's Office

AT THE KANSAS CITY FED

Truman stops here

Among the numerous tenants to lease space in the Federal Reserve Bank of Kansas City building, perhaps none was more fitting than the nation's 33rd president, a man well-known for his motto: The Buck Stops Here.

Although Harry Truman would eventually have an office at the Truman Library in his hometown of nearby Independence, his first post-White House office was in the Bank building.

Truman's arrival at the Bank for his first day in the new office in 1953 was recounted in a 1970 oral history interview of reporter Robert G. Nixon conducted by the Truman Library. After eight years with staff members eager to meet his every need, the former president came back to the Kansas City area eager to start doing things for himself – including getting himself to work.

"The morning after (Truman's) return to Independence, he got into his open car and drove the 15 miles or so into Kansas City. He parked his car in a parking lot adjacent to the Federal Reserve Building and walked across the street to the entrance where I was waiting," Nixon recalled.

Nixon, an International News Service correspondent who had covered the Truman White House, joined Truman and the former president's Secret Service agent as they walked into the Bank and took the elevator up to Truman's new office in the southwest corner of the 11th floor.

"The Secret Service agent was a few steps ahead, and, as usual, he started to open the door. The president said, in a loud voice, 'Please, wait. Let me open my own door. This is the first time in eight years that I have been able to open my own door, and I'm going to do it now.' The Secret

After leaving the White House, Harry Truman worked from an office located on the 11th floor of the Federal Reserve Bank of Kansas City. This photo was taken in May of 1954.

Service agent smiled and drew back. The president swung the door open, with a big, broad smile on his face, and we all trooped into his office," Nixon said.

Bank employees regularly saw Truman, by far the most prominent of the building's tenants.

Virginia Sutton, a Bank employee from 1945 until 1978 and the Bank's first female auditor, recalled receiving an unexpected but friendly response after addressing Truman as "president."

"He grabbed me by the arm and said, 'Young lady, I'm Harry,'" Sutton said during a 2006 interview.

The Truman that employees knew was one that matched what the general public saw. Former employees recall he was quick to open the door for the ladies. For Christmas, he gave the building's female elevator operators roses while he gave bottles of whiskey to some members of the Bank's security staff.

Although he often had lunch at downtown Kansas City locations, including the Kansas City Club and the Hotel Muehlebach, he was no stranger to the Bank's employee cafeteria.

"On occasion he would come up to the dining room and have lunch," said Wil Billington, retired executive vice president who joined the Bank in 1952, shortly before Truman's arrival the following year. "It was interesting to chat with him. The decisiveness you hear people talk about was clearly there."

Although Billington, an economist, was able to talk with Truman about business and the economy, it is the more personal discussions that he remembered most fondly.

"He was always upset about the reporters chastising his daughter for her musical performances," Billington said in a 2005 interview. "Things like that."

This more personal side of Truman was noted by others who met with the former president in what was then office 1107, one of four offices leased by Truman and his staff.

Philip C. Brooks, the first director of the Truman Library, had his first meeting with President Truman in the Bank office. Brooks recounted the experience while he was conducting a 1964 oral history interview on the Truman Library's behalf with Randall S. Jessee and his wife, who were friends of the 33rd president.

Harry Truman talks with reporters during a 1955 press conference in his office at the Federal Reserve Bank of Kansas City. Reporters regularly came to the Bank to talk with the former president.

Brooks said he was expecting a formal introduction as he waited in a reception room outside Truman's office.

"Pretty soon, as was normal - but I did not know it was normal - instead of being ushered into the august presence of the former president, Mr. Truman came walking out into that outer lobby with a smile on his face, and shook hands," Brooks said.

Truman was on his way to get some of his daughter's items out of storage and asked Brooks to come along. The two men left the building and began walking to another downtown location.

"This was the first experience I had had of walking with him on the street and having just odd people along with street say 'Hello, Harry,' and 'How are you, Harry,' and just shake hands. It was quite an experience."

As a part of her job in the audit department, Sutton recalled being sent to Truman's office to complete a furniture and equipment audit. While Truman's secretary was explaining that Sutton would need to come back at another time when the former president was out of the office, Truman appeared and invited Sutton in, telling her that he would assist with the audit.

"He turned chairs upside down, showed me the (inventory) numbers and he was reading them off to me," she said. "He helped me do my furniture and equipment audit."

Continued on next page

The job of a former president

Although Truman had time for personal greetings and his well-known public walks – he once said a daily two-mile walk before breakfast was the key to a long life – the former president certainly was not living the life of a leisurely retiree.

"He would have been reporting to work there (at the Bank) probably six days a week when he was in town," Ray Geselbracht, special assistant to the director at the Truman Presidential Library and Museum said in a 2005 interview.

Harry Truman autographs a copy of his memoirs for Barbara Bosley, a visitor to his office at the Bank. Much of Truman's time there was spent working on his memoirs.

From 1953 until the completion of the Truman Library in 1957, Geselbracht said Truman's days included the activities expected of a former president: There are photos of him meeting with reporters and other visitors; he was active in campaigning for his party's candidates and was busy responding to the numerous letters he received.

"He was meticulous about answering his correspondence," Geselbracht said. "I don't know that he let many letters go by unanswered."

In 1954, Truman was among the speakers at a dinner celebrating the Bank's 40th anniversary

Truman told the 400 business leaders attending the dinner at the Hotel Muehlebach that he had worked in two banks as a young man, but left the city to work on the farm.

"On the farm, I found that I was able-bodied but without finances," he said, "so I became a politician."

Much of Truman's time at his Bank office was spent working on his memoirs. Volume one, "Year of Decision," was published in 1955 while

"Years of Trial and Hope" was published the following year.

Truman was also busy planning for the Library.

Tom L. Evans, a Kansas City businessman, talked about the early planning process in a 1963 oral history interview with the Library.

According to a transcript of the interview, a group of Kansas City residents were working on plans to build the Truman Library on the campus of what was then known as the University of Kansas City – today, the University of Missouri-Kansas City. Supporters had picked a location along Rockhill Road; a site that Evans said in the transcript "couldn't have been a more beautiful spot."

A long-time friend of Truman's who often had lunch with the former president as a way of helping him adapt to the nuances of civilian life, Evans took Truman to the campus for a look.

"He wasn't very enthused; in fact, he wasn't enthused at all," Evans said.

Evans finally asked Truman about the site and the former president said he would prefer to locate the Library in Independence.

When asked why he had not previously mentioned Independence as a site for the Library, Truman told Evans that he "didn't want to cause any trouble." The former president had initially hoped to locate the Library on his family farm, but when that plan proved unfeasible, supporters began the push for the Rockhill Road location. The conversation with Evans may have been Truman's first opportunity to suggest Independence as the location.

Evans contacted Independence city officials, who started a process that eventually resulted in the city transferring the title to what was then called Slover Park, along with some neighboring properties, over to the Truman Library.

Truman broke ground on the privately funded library in the spring of 1955. He moved out of his office at the Bank and into the Library in 1957.

Although the Bank has now moved to a new building, Truman's connection to the Federal Reserve Bank of Kansas City continues. The nearly 500-piece Truman coin collection, featuring coins minted under each president since George Washington, is on loan to the Bank from the Truman Library and is on public display in the Bank's lobby.

Moving in

A year after the start of work, construction was nearing completion in June 1921. A story in the June 19, 1921 *Kansas City Journal* said workers were "in a heroic race against father time" to complete the building in time for an opening on Nov. 16, 1921 – the seven-year anniversary of the Bank's opening day.

"Kansas City has been witnessing for several months one of the greatest speed demonstrations of modern times," *The Journal* wrote.

The article goes on to describe the building:

"Every modern innovation and device for comfort has been planned for the interior equipment of the building. Not even the faintest hum of the city's manifold jarring and jangling noises will be heard

Bank Gov. Jo Zach Miller, Jr., with some of the many floral arrangements filling the lobby of the Bank headquarters building at 925 Grand on opening day, Nov. 16, 1921.

AIR CONDITIONING

The Federal Reserve Bank of Kansas City's headquarters was the first Kansas City office building to receive air conditioning. Although the Bank previously had air conditioning in its main banking floor, on the building's mezzanine level and in the vaults, the new system was expected to improve efficiency by improving the health of the Bank's staff and reducing cleaning costs.

"The (Bank's) Board of Directors found out today that by reason of existing equipment, including two big marine boilers, air conditioning could be extended over the entire structure, up to and including the 20th floor, for approximately $60,000. Otherwise the complete installation costs might have been two to three times that amount," *The Kansas City Star* wrote in its Feb. 23, 1934 edition.

According to the newspaper, a dozen years earlier the Bank had attempted to cool its lower floors with a then-cutting-edge feature known as "air washing."

"Only it didn't work," the article reads. "There were drafts, discomfort. The work space under the balconies seemed not to be reached by any eddy or freshened air. The years of experimentation that followed finally expanded the system into one of efficient air conditioning."

The new air conditioning, according to the newspaper, would keep the air generally 10 to 15 degrees cooler than the exterior temperature:

"In the new system, air will be taken in near the top of the building and mixed with retreated air on each floor. Each floor will have its air filters and single cooling unit. The retreated air will enter an office near the ceiling line and will be subject to control in each individual office."

The Jackson County Courthouse, then under construction just a few blocks away, was expected to be the city's second office building with air conditioning.

A letter to the Federal Reserve Bank of Cleveland responded to some questions about the success of an air conditioning system used in the Federal Reserve Bank of Kansas City.

November 10, 1934.

Mr. M. J. Fleming,
Deputy Governor,
Federal Reserve Bank of Cleveland,
Cleveland, Ohio.

Dear Mr. Fleming:

This will reply to your letter of November 5, addressed to Mr. Worthington, requesting information with reference to the cooling system at this office.

We now have in operation at the head office two cooling systems, one an ammonia compressor system, installed about five years ago at a cost of approximately $15,000, with a capacity of 50 tons, which serves the vault, ground floor, and balcony, including Board of Directors' rooms, the mechanism of which is located in the basement and is attached to the ducts originally installed as a ventilating system. The operating costs of such system are approximately $1,000 for cooling season. The second system is a steam-jet vacuum system which was installed during the past year, at a cost of approximately $75,000 exclusive of heating plant, and has a capacity of 300 tons and serves the upper fifteen floors of our building, aggregating approximately 165,000 sq. ft. of floor space, five floors of which are occupied by the bank and ten used as tenant floors. The major portion of the mechanical equipment of the latter system, consisting of a cooling tower and vacuum equipment, is located on the 21st floor and the roof, with a separate air cooling unit and fan on each floor. The equipment on the upper floor and roof is connected with our heating plant in the basement, and the cooling units and fans on each floor are connected with the principal equipment by air ducts and chilled water lines, a spare elevator shaft being utilized to house such cooling units and carry such lines.

Each floor has one centralized air duct running across the ceiling, with small lateral ducts branching off to either side. These ducts are exposed on the open floors, but run through the corridors of the tenant floors, the ceilings of which have been furred-in so the ducts are not exposed to view. The lateral ducts on these floors, as far as possible, have been run along the partition lines and have the appearance of beams, thereby supplying all enclosed spaces with conditioned air.

Both systems were designed and installed by C. H. Carr & Co., Engineers, Mutual Building, this city, who have done considerable work for us along heating, ventilating, and mechanical lines. The equipment was purchased from various manufacturers under specifications of Mr. Carr and installed under his supervision by various contractors.

While our experience with the latter system is somewhat limited, we are on the whole well pleased, and while the natural draft cooling tower originally

in the office because of a new and patented sound absorbing process, which is being installed in the walls and ceilings. All offices will be connected with a Pax interconnecting telephone system. The Bank will be equipped with a time recording apparatus. Other features include a complete gymnasium, assembly hall, café, kitchen, restrooms, hospital and special elevators for the banking force."

As work continued, the first employees moved into the building in July when auditing, accounting, analysis, filing and other departments moved to the building's second and third floors. Another group moved in August, and additional employees moved to the building in October. On Nov. 7, about $50 million in securities was moved from leased space at Eighth and Delaware streets to the new building in an armored car that made three trips. The night of Nov. 15, $14 million in currency, $20 million to $25 million in bonds and some $80 million in negotiable notes were moved from the R.A. Long Building to the new building's vault.

The move was described in a *Kansas City Star* article:

"Although transported only across Grand Avenue, the money and paper were moved in an armored van. To transport the money alone required nine trips. The van … stood at the Grand Avenue curb in front of the R.A. Long Building to be loaded. Then it drove to the alley (in) back of the new Bank building and directly into the basement of the Bank itself. A door closed and the van had been swallowed by the Bank."

That evening, Miller told a *Kansas City Journal* reporter for a story published the following morning that "there is not another example in the United States where such a large building has been constructed in such a short length of time."

On Nov. 16, the Bank opened for business in its new headquarters.

"It was scarcely businesslike, this opening today of the $4 million home of the ordinarily very businesslike Federal Reserve Bank," *The Kansas City Star* wrote in its Nov. 16, 1921 edition. "No clicking of dollar on dollar, no rattle of adding machines computing fabulous amounts. The first notes presented were not of the 'promise to pay' variety, but a rich chorus of music from young voices that flooded down from the mezzanine balcony as a greeting to the officers and directors of the Bank and to the throng in the lobby that included scores of men prominent in business and finance here.

An example of the detail work that adorns the exterior of the building at 925 Grand.

"The San Saban marble of the great main banking room, a room that rises three ordinary floors in height, formed a rich background for groupings of flowers and autumn leaves and flags; but nothing decorated the big room like the animated faces of scores of young Bank employees; the balconies were festooned with smiling clerks, and on the main floor, they elbowed men of business millions in appraising and applauding their new 'work home.'"

Among those in the lobby was W.P.G. Harding, the governor of the Federal Reserve Board in Washington, D.C. Harding was the guest of honor that evening at a banquet held at Kansas City's Muehlebach Hotel, where he told local bankers the economy was improving and talked about the Federal Reserve's unique structure. He also attended the first luncheon served on the building's 19th floor for the Bank's official staff and local bankers.

That morning's edition of *The Kansas City Times* published a brief editorial about the opening:

"The splendid Federal Reserve Bank building, which is formally opened today, is a monument first of all to the power and energy of this Southwestern territory it serves. Without the enormously productive industries of these states, there could have been no such building. But in addition, in a very real sense, the building is a monument to the vision and energy of Gov. J.Z. Miller, Jr., under whose direction it was constructed. Gov. Miller had the faith to believe that the resources of the District warranted the construction of a great office for the Reserve Bank. He had the force and capacity to win other men to his thinking and to see his vision realized.

"And the building is happily a symbol of the spirit of the Kansas City Bank. In the storm and stress of the last year and a half, the local Federal Reserve Bank has been a tower of strength to the whole Southwest. It has enabled a mobilizing of resources that saved the District from absolute disaster. The outcome has been an ample vindication of the wisdom with which the Bank was directed.

"A great institution, greatly housed. Cheers for Gov. Miller, its guiding genius!"

"The Building is Happily a symbol of the spirit of the Kansas City Bank."

Tenth District

BANK of KANSAS CITY

SPECULATION ABOUT WHICH CITIES MIGHT BE HOME TO *Branch offices* FOR THE NATION'S NEW REGIONAL FEDERAL RESERVE BANKS STARTED AS SOON AS THE RESERVE BANK *Organizing Committee* ANNOUNCED THE BOUNDARIES OF THE 12 FEDERAL RESERVE DISTRICTS ON APRIL 2, 1914.

And with that speculation came a second round of campaigns. Cities that had been unsuccessful in their previous efforts to win one of the regional offices retooled their efforts. Additionally, communities that had not sought the regional headquarters, such as Muskogee, Okla., in the Tenth District, also began to make a case for a Branch.

Although it would be seven months before the Federal Reserve Bank of Kansas City opened, and another three years before the Federal Reserve System began the widespread opening of Branches, newspaper accounts suggest the Tenth District Branch cities were fairly obvious.

An article about the characteristics of the Tenth Federal Reserve District published by *The Wall Street Journal* soon after the Reserve Bank Organizing Committee's announcement identified all three of the District's eventual Branch cities.

"Bankers who made a study of the probable operation of the new Federal Reserve System generally agree that the Federal Reserve Bank to be established in Kansas City for District No. 10 will open two branches, one at Omaha and another at Denver, soon after the parent institution is in operation," reads an article in the newspaper's April 25, 1914 edition.

Although the article says it is unlikely the Bank would open a Branch in Oklahoma, which had only been a state for seven years, it does say that if conditions do merit a Branch to serve the District's southern communities "a bank may be necessary at Oklahoma City."

The Branch question

The issue of Branches raised a somewhat difficult question for the nation's new central bank.

Some of the public expected to see Branch locations opening almost immediately after the Federal Reserve System became operational.

The new regional Banks, however, were uninterested in opening additional offices, and taking on increased costs, without a clear demonstration that the Branches were necessary to serve their Districts.

The Federal Reserve Act offered little guidance.

"Each Federal Reserve Bank shall establish Branch Banks within the Federal Reserve District in which it is located."

Although the Act does spell out some provisions for Branch governance, it offers no criteria or requirements for opening Branch offices. Instead, it offers only a sentence that was often pointed to by those urging a quick opening of Branch offices:

"Each Federal Reserve Bank shall establish Branch Banks within the Federal Reserve District in which it is located."

It is clear that the issue of Branch offices was a concern from the System's opening.

Jo Zach Miller, Jr., told Denver bankers that the city was in line to receive a Branch during what was likely his first trip there as chairman of the Federal Reserve Bank of Kansas City.

"His assurance that Denver will get the Branch was received with great enthusiasm by the 250 bankers and business men whom he addressed at the Kaiserhof Hotel," reads an account in the March 6, 1915 *Denver News.*

Miller was far from the first to raise the issue of a Denver Branch. In an April 3, 1914 *Rocky Mountain News* story about the selection of the 12 Reserve Bank Districts, Colorado banker Gordon Jones, a future director of the Federal Reserve Bank of Kansas City, said he had already been assured that Denver would receive a Branch by no less a source than Treasury Secretary William McAdoo.

The first Branch of a Federal Reserve Bank opened on Sept. 10, 1915, in New Orleans – a city that many were surprised was not selected for a regional headquarters. The Branch of the Federal Reserve Bank of Atlanta was almost immediately successful, according to the Federal Reserve Board's 1915 annual report. The report, however, follows its comments about New Orleans with a paragraph suggesting Branches would not be viable elsewhere in the near future:

"Investigation and experience have seemed to show that, at least for some years to come, the organization of Branches with completely equipped offices, vaults, and the like, and with a full staff of salaried officials, will be too heavy an expense for most of the Reserve Banks."

That position changed in the following years.

In his 1922 paper, "The Establishment and Scope of the Branches of the Federal Reserve Banks," E.R. Fancher, then-governor of the Federal Reserve Bank of Cleveland, says that the Bank's increased responsibilities after the United States entered World War I boosted earnings and provided funding that allowed for the opening of Branches.

There was, perhaps, another reason that contributed to the decision.

Increasing public frustration about the Branch issue meant the Federal Reserve also faced the potential for legislation that would require Branch openings. Instead, the Federal Reserve Act was amended to clarify some of the Branch issues in June 1917, and Branch openings soon followed with five Branch openings, including one in the Tenth District.

Federal Reserve Bank of Kansas City Gov. Jo Zach Miller, Jr., led the Bank during the establishment of Branches in Denver, Oklahoma City and Omaha.

OMAHA

According to Jess Worley's unpublished history of the Federal Reserve Bank of Kansas City, the Omaha Clearing House banks sent a letter to the Federal Reserve Bank of Kansas City seeking a Branch in June 1917.

Charles Sawyer, chairman of the Bank's Board of Directors, and Miller, who by this time had become governor of the Bank, the title similar to today's president, traveled to Omaha on July 10 to explore the issue. The pair arrived in Omaha in time for dinner and met with bankers for two hours before returning to Kansas City by train that evening.

In an apparent attempt to influence the Bank, *The Omaha World-Herald* published a lengthy editorial listing the city's merits and noting its growth in the years since its failed bid for a regional Bank headquarters:

"Only two or three years ago it was Omaha's proudest boast that though it was the 41st city of the country in population, it was 16th in bank clearings.

"So rapidly is Omaha and its tributary territory developing that this boast is already outgrown. Omaha is today 30th in population. And it is 13th in bank clearings."

Omaha, an important rail hub in its own right, made a strong case for winning a regional Bank office in 1914, so it was not surprising when the city was selected for the first Federal Reserve Bank of Kansas City Branch office.

Despite the hopes of some, Miller did not use the July 10 meeting to announce the formation of an Omaha Branch. The city's bankers, however, left the meeting encouraged.

"I feel that our meeting was a success, and although nothing was definitely determined, I think several questions which have been bothering us are satisfactorily settled," Luther Drake, president of the Merchants National Bank, told *The Omaha World-Herald* for its July 11, 1917 edition. "I think there is no question but what the Branch will be established in this city, but at what date, I cannot say."

It would come quickly.

The Federal Reserve Bank of Kansas City's Board approved the Omaha Branch during a meeting two days later. The Federal Reserve Board in Washington, D.C., approved the request, a step that was perhaps a matter of mere formality, on July 18. The Branch opened on Sept. 4, 1917, in the Farnam Building.

"… Omaha has always been an important banking town."

It is not surprising that the process leading to the opening of the Branch moved rapidly. From the time Kansas City was announced as the regional headquarters, bankers thought it inevitable that Omaha would get a Branch after being passed over by the Reserve Bank Organizing Committee three years earlier. In 1914, many in Omaha believed their community was in line for a regional Bank instead of a Branch.

Omaha's 1914 presentation touted the city's role as a regional agricultural hub, its extensive connections with banks to the west and its rail history.

"(W)e would state that from the earliest settlement of this western country, Omaha has always been an important banking town," the Omaha contingent said in its submission to the Committee. "Every bank which came into existence in the territories … west of us found it necessary to keep an account in Omaha.

"This was occasioned not only because it was the end of overland travel before the railroads came into being, but also for the fact that the first overland railroad made its start from Omaha, at an initial point fixed by President Abraham Lincoln."

Interestingly, the Omaha presentation suggests that the city saw its chief rivals as nearby Lincoln and, unexpectedly, Denver, instead of Kansas City. Although the District proposed in Kansas City included Omaha, the Omaha District's southern boundary stopped short of Kansas City, an apparent recognition that Omaha bankers believed Kansas City, nearly twice Omaha's size at that time, would win one of the Banks.

As officials prepared to announce the location of the 12 Federal Reserve Bank cities, Omaha held out hope it would be selected. This cartoon from the April 1, 1914 edition of The Omaha Daily Bee *seemed to suggest Omaha felt its hopes had been raised only to be dashed. When the Reserve Bank cities were announced the following day, Omaha was not selected, forcing the city leaders to turn their attention toward winning a Branch office.*

Omaha's focus on Denver instead of Kansas City was also evident in coverage of the issue by the city's newspapers. *The Omaha Daily Bee* wrote only a brief story about the Reserve Bank Organizing Committee's Kansas City hearing and buried it at the bottom of the paper's second page under the headline "Kansas City Wants Bank." The later Denver hearing, meanwhile, was front page news under a headline proclaiming "Bankers of Denver Fail to Make Case."

Although Omaha bankers may not have seen Kansas City as a rival, Kansas Citians apparently felt otherwise.

As it did in much of the rest of the region, the Kansas City Clearing House sent a contingent to meet with a group from the Omaha Clearing House, seeking support for Kansas City's bid during a Jan. 11, 1914 meeting. Although Kansas City was successful in gaining support in other regions, Omaha bankers were unwilling to relinquish their own effort for a Regional Bank.

"The representatives of both cities are agreed that there are no serious obstacles ahead that will prevent either one of these two cities from each being the headquarters of a regional Bank, the important commercial and geographical location of each being so obvious that only an unnatural division of the current of trade could prevent the end desired," the Omaha group said in a statement issued after the meeting.

As might be expected, the announcement of Kansas City as the headquarters of a District encompassing Nebraska drew an angry response. Newspaper accounts suggested Omaha bankers were far angrier with the Committee than those in some of the other cities that were not selected.

"Nothing in the world but politics governed the decision by which the Federal Reserve Banks were located," Henry W. Yates, president of the Nebraska National Bank told a reporter. "It is disgraceful – it's an outrage."

A similar tone was voiced by other bankers and the state's Congressional delegation.

In reaction to the decision, some banks in both Nebraska and Wyoming petitioned to become part of the Chicago Federal Reserve District. The request was denied.

By the summer of 1917, however, the Omaha bankers had apparently overcome their anger. They moved aggressively to secure a Branch for the city and were pleased when they learned it would open.

"I am naturally delighted to know the Branch bank will be located in Omaha," J.H. Millard, president of Omaha National Bank and a senator at the time, told *The Omaha World-Herald* for its July 12, 1917 edition. "All the Omaha bankers think it will be of great benefit to this city and to the entire state as well as the state of Wyoming. It is just the thing we needed."

The Omaha Branch of the Federal Reserve Bank of Kansas City opened in the Farnam Building at 13th and Farnam streets.

DENVER

The Denver Clearing House Association moved almost as quickly as their counterparts in Omaha, submitting their request for a Branch in July 1917. The Association, like their counterparts in New Orleans when seeking that city's Branch, agreed to pay for any financial shortfalls the Branch might suffer.

"The Denverites were so convinced of the Federal Reserve's value to Denver that the Association's member banks volunteered to cover any deficit in operations. The (Bank's) Board unanimously agreed in August to establish a Branch in Denver," reads a 1968 account of the Branch's history.

Denver bankers believed that by not being selected to house the regional headquarters, their city also was almost guaranteed a Branch office. John C. Mitchell, president of the Denver National Bank, discussed the situation with a *Kansas City Post* reporter while Mitchell was in Kansas City to sign the charter incorporating the Federal Reserve Bank of Kansas City.

"Denver hated to lose. But after the first few days of disappointment, the feeling of defeat was replaced by a determination to make the Kansas City District one of the strongest in the country," Mitchell said. "And then, besides, we are to have a Branch of Kansas City's Bank."

The Denver Branch opened on Jan. 14, 1918, in the Interstate Trust Building at the corner of 16th and Lawrence streets.

"The Denver Branch of the Federal Reserve Bank of Kansas City was formally opened yesterday, and while some business was transacted, the day was given over to receiving callers as representatives of practically every other bank in Denver and many from out of town called to offer their

The Arch of Welcome on 17th Street in Denver. Denver officials felt confident their city would be selected as the site of a Branch office of the Federal Reserve Bank of Kansas City.

(1)-10610-Arch of Welcome, 17th St. E.S.E. from railway station, Denver, Colo.   Copyright Underwood & Underwood. U-118683

congratulations on the installation of this Branch," reads an article in the Jan. 15, 1918 edition of *The Rocky Mountain News.*

The Denver Branch was one of 10 Federal Reserve Bank Branches opening in 1918, giving the System a total of 16 Branches by the end of the year. The System's relatively quick transition from reluctance toward the idea of Branches to an embrace of the Branch model in only a couple of years is not surprising. The Branches improved the efficiency of the regional Reserve Banks, giving them a direct connection to areas often far from the regional headquarters. The Branches also offered the potential for increased System membership by commercial banks in the area. This increase in membership, in turn, could bring greater stability to the entire System.

68TH CONGRESS, 1ST SESSION.

H. J. RES. 169

IN THE HOUSE OF REPRESENTATIVES.

JANUARY 31, 1924.

Mr. VAILE introduced the following joint resolution; which was referred to the Committee on Banking and Currency and ordered to be printed.

JOINT RESOLUTION

Authorizing the Federal Reserve Bank of Kansas City to invest its funds in the construction of a building for its branch office at Denver, Colorado.

1 *Resolved by the Senate and House of Representatives*

2 *of the United States of America in Congress assembled,*

3 That the Federal Reserve Bank of Kansas City is hereby

4 authorized to invest in the construction of a building for

5 its branch office at Denver, Colorado, on lots heretofore

6 acquired for that purpose, a sum not to exceed $650,000

7 out of its paid-in capital stock and surplus.

The Denver Branch opened on Jan. 14, 1918, in the Interstate Trust Building at the corner of 16th and Lawrence streets. Within a few years, approval was granted for the Branch to build its own office at 1111 17th St.

OKLAHOMA CITY

With two Branches of the Federal Reserve Bank of Kansas City operational, 1919 saw four communities in the Tenth Federal Reserve District vying to house a third Branch.

After receiving applications from both Oklahoma City and Tulsa during its June 19, 1919 meeting, the Bank's Board of Directors scheduled a hearing for July 24 to hear from both cities as well as presentations from two other communities that had previously filed applications: Wichita, Kan., and Lincoln, Neb.

The corner of Third and Harvey in downtown Oklahoma City was cleared to make way for the Federal Reserve Bank of Kansas City's Oklahoma City Branch office.

Newspaper accounts of the event, which was held in the White Room of Kansas City's Baltimore Hotel, reveal an atmosphere that was reminiscent of what the Reserve Bank Organizing Committee encountered five years earlier during its tour to determine the Reserve Bank cities.

"With all the energy of auctioneers, Tulsa, Oklahoma City and Wichita ran up their bids yesterday for the favors of the district Federal Reserve Board," reads coverage of the event in the July 25, 1919 edition of *The Kansas City Journal.*

While the two Oklahoma cities and Wichita wanted to serve the southern portion of the Tenth Federal Reserve District, Lincoln based its case on "seeing Nebraska business first," and suggested it would serve banks south of the Platte River and in northern Kansas. The Bank's willingness to hear the Lincoln presentation may have been a mere courtesy. With its location near Omaha, and suggesting it could serve Kansas counties that were already served by the Kansas City office, Lincoln had virtually no chance of receiving a Branch.

The southern cities, meanwhile, fell victim to the same issue that plagued many cities in their efforts to win one of the regional Banks in 1914. Their arguments focused more on their superiority than on how their community was a factor in the flow of the region's business.

While Oklahoma City noted that many of the state's banks petitioned for the city to host the Branch, the presentation also talked about the city's advantages over Tulsa.

The Tulsa presentation, meanwhile, talked about the city's growth and its role in world oil markets, and the Wichita presentation included comments suggesting that everything from Tulsa and Oklahoma City was "on the way to Wichita" before heading on to Kansas City.

At its Sept. 25 meeting, the Bank's Board of Directors took up the Branch issue. A motion by Director Harrison W. Gibson of Muskogee, Okla., to recommend to the Federal Reserve Board that a Branch be established in one of the two Oklahoma communities failed by a 3-6 margin with Gibson joined by Kansas Citians Col. F.W. Fleming and Board Chairman Asa E. Ramsay in support of creating a Branch in Oklahoma.

The vote was followed by a motion from Director Thomas C. Byrne of Omaha, Neb., not to open a Branch in Oklahoma. It was approved along the same lines as the previous vote.

According to Worley, the second motion was made for two reasons:

- The original Reserve Banks were located not in regard to state boundaries, but, instead, to relate to the natural course of business;

- The presentations by each of the three cities "were based largely upon their claimed superiority over other contending cities, whereas the contentions should have been based upon the commercial fitness to serve a territory not already fully served by the Bank or existing Bank Branch."

"We'll have to fight for it as we have had to fight for everything else the city ever got, but we are going to Win."

While Byrne made the motion, it is noteworthy that the opposition to an Oklahoma Branch was led by Director Willis J. Bailey, an Atchison, Kan. banker who had previously had a high-profile political career in Kansas. Bailey had been both a Congressman from the state and had also served a term as the state's governor. Although no record remains on the Board's discussion of the Oklahoma Branch issue, newspaper accounts later indicated Bailey was the primary opponent to an Oklahoma Branch. Given his background, it is perhaps likely that he favored a Wichita Branch instead.

The Bank's decision promoted a quick response from Oklahomans. Oklahoma Sen. Robert L. Owen, co-sponsor of the Federal Reserve Act in 1913, penned what newspaper accounts called "a strong letter of protest" to W.P.G. Harding, chairman of the Federal Reserve Board, expressing his anger at the decision.

Meanwhile, the Oklahoma City Clearing House was among the groups sending telegrams to the Federal Reserve Board seeking a hearing on the issue.

"We'll have to fight for it as we have had to fight for everything else the city ever got, but we are going to win," Daniel W. Hogan, president of the Oklahoma City Clearing House Association told *The Daily Oklahoman* for a Sept. 27, 1919 story. "I do not expect to see the Branch established immediately, for there is much opposition to be overcome and there are many difficulties in the matter of detail. But within the next year or two, Oklahoma City will have that bank."

The Sept. 25 vote was the second time the Bank's Board of Directors had rejected the idea of opening an Oklahoma Branch. In 1917, after receiving bids from Oklahoma City, Tulsa and Muskogee, the Bank's Board decided to postpone any decision on a Branch in Oklahoma until after Nebraska and Colorado Branches were established.

The second rejection only compounded the frustration felt by many in Oklahoma City who believed their city had been promised a Branch years earlier. According to numerous newspaper accounts from the period, Oklahomans said that at least three Kansas City bankers in 1914 promised that Oklahoma City would receive a Federal Reserve Bank Branch if the state's bankers supported Kansas City's bid to house the regional Bank headquarters.

The Federal Reserve Bank of Kansas City's Oklahoma City Branch opened in the Continental Building on the corner of Second Street and Broadway in 1920. Soon, officials made plans to construct a new Branch building. Bank Gov. Willis J. Bailey, (in bow tie) presided during the 1922 ceremony at the corner of Third and Harvey streets.

Although the Kansas City bankers would have no say on where a Federal Reserve Branch would be located, it is possible that their promises influenced Oklahomans. The Sooner State strongly supported Kansas City's effort – 85 percent of the state's bankers who voted in the Reserve Bank Organizing Committee's poll favored Kansas City, instead of Oklahoma City or Tulsa, as their first choice for the regional Reserve Bank headquarters.

An undated photo of Oklahoma City Branch employees. The Bank's name can be seen on the window.

The anger toward Kansas City was voiced by many Oklahoma City bankers and especially apparent in an editorial titled, "Justice for Oklahoma," published by *The Daily Oklahoman* two weeks before a Federal Reserve Board hearing on the issue.

"Probably there has never been an act in the history of the Federal Reserve banking system so extraordinary as the act of the Tenth District Reserve Board at Kansas City in persistently and arbitrarily refusing to grant a Branch Reserve Bank in Oklahoma City," begins the Oct. 7, 1920 editorial – a lengthy piece that makes numerous accusations related to Kansas City's motives and is even critical of the Bank's then-planned construction of a new headquarters.

Delegations from both Oklahoma City and Tulsa traveled to Washington, D.C., for an Oct. 21 meeting where the Federal Reserve Board reviewed applications and heard presentations from both cities.

"Oklahoma City seems sure to win the bank now."

After reviewing the documents, the Federal Reserve Board sent a telegram to Kansas City asking the Bank to forward to the Board various reports about the movement of commerce in the southern portion of the District, indicating that a Branch would open in one of the two Oklahoma cities. On Nov. 26, the Federal Reserve Board then sent a letter to Oklahoma banks outside of Oklahoma City and Tulsa asking their preference on the Branch's location.

"In order that this Branch may be located with a view to the interests of the territory to be served, the Board desires from you an unbiased statement indicating your preference as between the two cities named," reads part of the letter.

Word of the vote was good news in Oklahoma City, where a key part of the campaign to win the Branch was a petition signed by Oklahoma banks.

"Oklahoma City seems sure to win the bank now," Frank P. Johnson, chairman of the Oklahoma City effort, told *The Daily Oklahoman* for a Nov. 30, 1919 story. "More than 200 member banks in the state endorsed Oklahoma City when we presented the petition to the Board, and I am certain they will return the same decision now. The vote was more than two to one for us. We have been in close touch with all the banks and can rely upon them fully."

The Federal Reserve Board issued a press release announcing Oklahoma City's selection on Dec. 17, 1919, and the Branch opened on Aug. 2, 1920, in the Continental Building at the corner of Second Street and Broadway.

New buildings

Although the Branches opened in leased office space, the Bank worked quickly to move each into Bank-owned facilities.

In Omaha, the Bank paid $165,000 in early 1920 to purchase the five-story Farnam Building, where the Branch had been a tenant.

"a financial Rock of Gibraltar"

Each of the Federal Reserve Bank of Kansas City's Branches was in a new building in the early 1920s. In the years that followed, Denver and Omaha moved to new buildings while Oklahoma City expanded its historic structure.

"Some remodeling of the quarters which the Branch occupies has been made, and further important changes are contemplated, which when completed, will result in the Branch utilizing 15,300 square-feet of the building purchased," reads an account of the Branch's history written in April 1921.

The Branch moved to its second home at 17th and Dodge streets in 1925, and moved for a third time in 1986 after construction was completed on the current Branch office at 2201 Farnam St.

For the Branches in Denver and Oklahoma City, the Bank's Board of Directors voted to purchase lots in both cities on June 23, 1921.

The Bank paid $65,000 to purchase lots at the southwest corner of Third and Harvey streets in Oklahoma City, but had some difficulty in completing the purchase of property in Denver. In August, the Bank's Board had selected a location in downtown Denver for $350,000. The figure was $200,000 more than the Bank had planned to spend, according to Worley's unpublished history. Apparently because of the high cost, the Federal Reserve Board sent the Bank a letter in September instructing it to instead obtain neighboring lots at the corner of 18th and Curtis streets for $100,000, which was later purchased.

Work on constructing a three-story Oklahoma City Branch office started in 1922. The building, which *The Daily Oklahoman* called "a financial rock of Gibraltar," opened in 1923. An addition to the building was completed in 1962.

Omaha
17TH AND DODGE STREETS
1925 - 1986

Denver
1111 17TH STREET
1925 - 1968

Oklahoma City
THIRD AND HARVEY STREETS
1923 - CURRENT
(With an addition in 1962)

Tragedy

In Denver, the Branch continued to operate out of leased space in 1922 as work was set to begin on the construction of a new Branch office.

Conditions in the Interstate Trust Building were difficult. Former Bank Director Bailey, who became the Bank's governor in 1922, once noted that when he visited the Denver Branch on a day when the mercury fell to -14 degrees, "…the employees had to wear wraps, as it was impossible to heat the building."

The building was also too small, forcing the Branch to store some of its currency at member banks and at the nearby U.S. Mint, utilizing an armored truck for transit back and forth. The shortfalls of the arrangement became tragically clear at 10:30 a.m. Dec. 18, 1922, when four men, including two firing sawed-off shotguns, robbed a Federal Reserve truck parked outside the Mint.

It was one of the most infamous crimes in U.S. history.

"In the five minutes it took the bandits to pull off their record-breaking crime, pandemonium ruled, with the alarm bell in the Mint going continuously, scores of people rushing from nearby buildings, shots ringing out in a drumfire that seemed as if it must take many lives," reads *The Denver Post's* coverage of the incident.

Although newspaper accounts say as many as 50 Mint security guards returned fire, the bandits got away with $200,000 in $5 bills. Killed in the attack was Denver

Armored cars such as this one were used by the Federal Reserve Bank of Kansas City in the early 1920s, and at the time of the Denver Mint robbery.

Branch security officer Charles T. Linton, a Branch employee since its 1918 opening. Linton, who returned three shots before being fatally wounded, was proclaimed a hero in a drawing on the front page of the Dec. 19, 1922 *Denver Post.*

Linton's wife told *The Post* that the officer had a premonition he would soon lose his life.

"Only a few days before he told me that he wanted to die on his feet, instantly," Eliza Linton said. "He said he wished the end would come from a shot or heart failure. He did not die instantly, but he did die … doing his duty."

In the aftermath of the attack, Denver businesses and banks refused to accept $5 bills, apparently in hopes of discouraging their use. The robbery vehicle, a Buick, was found four weeks later with the frozen and gunshot-riddled body of convicted criminal Nick Trainor inside. A year later, $80,000 of the missing bills were recovered in St. Paul, Minn., but no one was ever arrested or charged.

"We hope the robbery will hasten the building of our bank and vaults so that money shipped to us may be delivered to us directly rather than to the United States Mint first and then to us," Denver Branch Manager Charles A. Burkhardt told reporters after the attack. "We are doing everything we can to have the bank built as soon as possible, for we certainly need it."

The new office at 1111 17th St. opened three years later in 1925. Its design was essentially identical to the Oklahoma City structure.

The Branch stayed in that building until 1968 when construction was completed on the building at 1020 16th St., which remains its home.

OMAHA *Branch*
2201 FARNAM STREET

DENVER *Branch*
1020 16TH STREET

FEDERAL RESERVE BANK

Current

OKLAHOMA CITY *Branch*
226 DEAN A. MCGEE AVENUE

Branch Buildings

Tenth District

BANK *of* KANSAS CITY

THE POSITION OF *president* OF THE FEDERAL RESERVE BANK OF KANSAS CITY HAS PROVEN TO BE ONE OF THE MOST *stable leadership* POSITIONS IN THE ENTIRE FEDERAL RESERVE SYSTEM.

At the time the Bank moved to its new home at 1 Memorial Drive, Thomas M. Hoenig was the Bank's eighth president since its opening on Nov. 16, 1914. Only the Richmond Federal Reserve Bank, with seven presidents, has had fewer leaders during the same span. But unlike Richmond, which, astonishingly, had only two presidents during its first 46 years, the Kansas City Bank's first leaders were the ones with the briefest tenures. Each of the last four Kansas City Bank presidents has held the post for more than 14 years.

That is not to downplay the importance of the early presidents.

In fact, Jo Zach Miller, Jr., who served in the position that became Bank president for less than seven years, is remembered today as the Bank's founder. Miller's leadership and vision during the Bank's early years; the opening of its Branches in Omaha, Denver and Oklahoma City; and the construction of the building at 925 Grand Blvd. very literally established the Bank's foundation.

Similarly, each of his successors has built upon that foundation. They've led the Bank through the challenges of their times and, despite their varied backgrounds, brought to the job a strong commitment to the Bank and the Tenth Federal Reserve District.

The most telling sign of their success is perhaps that, nearly a century after the Bank's founding, so few have held the job.

Charles Manville Sawyer, Governor, 1914-1916

Charles Manville Sawyer occupies a unique place in the history of the Federal Reserve Bank of Kansas City. Although he was the first to hold the position that would later become Bank president, it is his successor, and not Sawyer, who is today referred to as the Bank's "first president."

Sawyer was one of eight children born to Lewis and Salanda Sawyer on a farm near Streator, Ill., and the only one who did not attend college, according to William E. Connelley's 1918 book "A Standard History of Kansas and Kansans."

At the influence of a brother-in-law, 21-year-old Sawyer moved to the northwestern Kansas town of Norton in 1887 and soon became cashier of the First National Bank.

"During that period, he gained a wide acquaintance with the people of northwestern Kansas and came in touch with the early settlers during the series of hard years which beset them," Connelly writes.

He left the job to become a national bank examiner, a position that Connelley says provided Sawyer with "exceptional opportunities for acquaintance and association with bankers all over the state."

In 1897, he returned to the Norton bank as president and became involved with a number of northwestern Kansas banks. He was president of the Kansas Bankers Association in 1898 and was also a member of the executive council of the American Bankers Association.

The banking connections were likely a factor when Kansas Gov. George H. Hodges appointed Sawyer the state's bank commissioner in 1913. They were clearly one reason he was selected as the first governor of the Federal Reserve Bank of Kansas City the following year.

The decision, however, was also influenced by some of the difficulties the Bank's Board of Directors faced by being able to pay only a relatively modest salary to Bank officers.

According to a partial transcript of the Bank's first Board meeting on Oct. 16, 1914, Director Willis J. Bailey, along with many local bankers, favored Peter W. Goebel for the job.

Goebel, who would later become president of the American Bankers Association, was at that

Charles Sawyer had served as president of the Kansas Bankers Association and as the Kansas banking commissioner before being selected as the first governor of the Federal Reserve Bank of Kansas City.

time president of the Kansas City Clearing House Association. He'd served as president of the large Commercial National Bank of Kansas City, Kan., since its opening and had been instrumental in the effort to win the regional Reserve Bank for Kansas City.

"I have been and am favorable to the selection of Mr. Goebel as governor, but he will not accept the position for less than $10,000," Bailey told the rest of the Board. "I have known him for years; and I know his ability, and I know the bank would be safe with him as governor. He will not take it at $7,500 a year. He has told me to say that to this Board."

The salary limit was partially a result of some of the complexities of the young Federal Reserve System.

Jo Zach Miller, Jr., as Bank chairman, had a salary set at $7,500 by the Federal Reserve Board in Washington, D.C. Since the governor would report to Miller, the Kansas City Board felt it inappropriate to offer a higher salary to the governor.

R.H. Malone, a Bank director from Denver, told the Board about a meeting he had attended with the directors of the Federal Reserve Bank of Cleveland and Federal Reserve officials in Washington. The Cleveland Bank wanted to offer a salary of at least $12,000 to its governor.

"And the (Washington) Board said 'they ought to work for less. We want someone to work for patriotism and honor and good of the government rather than for financial compensation,'" Malone said. "The impression left on me was honor rather than compensation."

Miller told the Board some had expressed surprise that he was willing to accept a comparatively meager salary for his job. He indicated that he had discussed the issue with Federal Reserve officials in Washington, who told him "they were not buying anybody's time for its commercial value … everybody had to sacrifice something for the good of the country."

Miller's comment essentially brought the discussion to a close and the Board approved a motion to limit the governor's salary to $7,500 annually. The decision eliminated Goebel from consideration, and Miller raised Sawyer's name for discussion.

"I understand he has given Kansas a very efficient service," Miller said. "I will say this: One of the

"Everybody had to Sacrifice something for the good of the country."

things the Washington Board indicated was that we … should endeavor to the best of (our) ability to induce the state banks to come in. Now along those lines, I think Mr. Sawyer would serve us very well. Half the business this bank will get will come from Kansas."

The Board quickly voted to hire Sawyer.

Charles Sawyer and his wife, May Holmes Sawyer, in their later years. After leaving the Kansas City Fed, the Sawyers moved to California.

THE SWITCH

Little is known about Sawyer's tenure as Bank governor other than it was soon apparent that Miller and Sawyer were better suited for each other's jobs.

In his unpublished Bank history, Jess Worley explains, "the responsibility that should be assumed by the governor in carrying out the operating end of the Bank was such that it required someone of both large banking experience and of resourcefulness and executive ability."

Although the Board was sometimes portrayed as unclear about the positions when it made the decision to hire Sawyer, comments made during the Oct. 16, 1914 meeting suggest otherwise.

Bailey described Goebel to the other directors as "a natural executive officer" and, as they prepared to vote on offering the position to Sawyer, noted the differences between the two men.

"Mr. Sawyer will fill a different position than Mr. Goebel would have filled," Bailey said.

At a Jan. 4, 1916 meeting, the Kansas City Board appointed Miller to the governor position. The job switch was completed when the Federal Reserve Board later approved a recommendation by the Kansas City Board to name Sawyer the Bank's new chairman.

Sawyer served as chairman until his term expired in December 1917.

An article in the Dec. 25, 1917 edition of *The Kansas City Star* announcing Sawyer's departure from the Board said he would "probably engage in some private enterprise, the nature of which he was not yet ready to disclose."

Not much is known of Sawyer's life after leaving the Bank. He did eventually retire to Hollywood, Calif., and was among several prominent Kansans who attended a luncheon that was featured in the March 21, 1928 edition of *The Los Angeles Times*. Other luncheon attendees included Bailey, who was then governor of the Federal Reserve Bank of Kansas City, and Hodges, the former Kansas governor who had appointed Sawyer to the position of Kansas bank commissioner.

It is possible that Sawyer was never again in Kansas City after his departure from the Bank. Portraits of both Sawyer and Miller by French artist Charles Bennell were unveiled at the Bank in April 1922, but Sawyer did not attend the ceremony. Sawyer, in fact, sat for Bennell's portrait in Los Angeles.

Sawyer's obituary, which appeared in the Sept. 28, 1950 edition of *The Los Angeles Times*, noted he was the "retired first president of the Federal Reserve Bank, Kansas City." He was 84.

Four generations of the Sawyer family are pictured in this 1922 photo. Charles Sawyer (standing) is joined by his daughter Francis Sawyer Folks. Seated are Charles' father, Lewis Manville Sawyer, and Charles' granddaughter Nancy.

Jo Zach Miller, Jr., who would later lead the founding of the Federal Reserve Bank of Kansas City, as a young man growing up in Texas.

JO ZACH MILLER, JR., CHAIRMAN, 1914-1916; GOVERNOR, 1916-1922

The man who is today remembered as the first president of the Federal Reserve Bank of Kansas City was actually not its first president.

He was, however, the right man for the job – someone able to overcome what critics saw as the sizable challenge of establishing a regional headquarters for a new central bank in a nation that had not warmed to two previous attempts at creating such an institution.

Miller, a self-made success story, had already proven that he was up for the challenge. Left fatherless before he was a teen and later diagnosed by doctors who predicted an early grave, Miller was a healthy, self-made millionaire by the age of 51. Then, after a successful career in commercial banking, he agreed to receive a relatively meager salary as compensation for leading the Federal Reserve Bank of Kansas City, a position that would force him to shed the investments in banks and financial institutions that had built much of his fortune.

By the time of his departure eight years later, the Federal Reserve Bank of Kansas City was well-established.

Miller oversaw the opening of Branch offices in the key cities of Denver, Oklahoma City and Omaha. Meanwhile, the Kansas City Bank moved out of its rented office space and into a newly built headquarters reaching a then-skyscraping 21 stories and able to serve the Bank for decades. The Bank's staff grew similarly under his direction, from an opening day roster of 15 employees, many hired directly by Miller, to some 500 workers at the time of his departure.

Although he had spent three decades in commercial banking prior to his stint with the Federal Reserve, and would be involved in several business ventures in his later years, Miller's tenure at the Federal Reserve Bank of Kansas City resulted in his being referred to simply as "the governor" for decades to come. At the end of his life he would be appropriately lauded as "the directing force" of the Federal Reserve Bank of Kansas City.

Texas roots

Jo Zach Miller, Jr., was born April 16, 1863, on a farm southeast of Austin, Texas, in rural Bastrop County. His parents, William Addison Miller and Amanda Priscilla Elliott had married in Kentucky in 1859 and came to the Lone Star State only a few months prior to the outbreak of the Civil War. Soon after Jo Zach's birth, with William in poor health and considered an invalid, the family moved to nearby Belton, Texas, where William was able to work as a teacher and a land surveyor. Briefly, before his death at age 33, William also became involved in a mercantile business combined with a private bank called Miller and Chamberlin, later known as Miller Brothers.

After William's passing, Jo Zach, then 11, was raised by Amanda with help from William's brother Col. Joseph Zachary Miller, the man for whom the boy had fittingly been named. Amanda and Joseph also assumed responsibility for Miller Brothers where Jo Zach spent many of his days prior to attending St. Louis University in 1880.

After Jo Zach returned to Texas from school at age 21, he joined his uncle in establishing the Belton National Bank with Jo Zach serving as its manager and Joseph its president.

Joseph Miller, by this time, was a well-known Texas banker, holding positions with several banking

Col. Joseph Zachary Miller, the man for whom Jo Zach Miller, Jr., was named, raised his nephew from the age of 11. When the younger Miller was grown, the two became partners in establishing the Belton National Bank in Texas.

organizations, including serving as president of the Texas National Bankers Association from 1895 to 1900. His business interests, however, extended beyond banking. An article in the Sept. 25, 1886 edition of *The St. Louis Globe Democrat* listed him as one of the wealthiest men in the Lone Star State. Texas newspaper articles from that period note he was president of the Hearne, Belton and Northwest Railroad Company and had previously been involved with a wholesale hat business. He also served as temporary chair of the Texas Prohibition Convention.

In his 1920 obituary, Joseph Miller, who served as a colonel in the Confederate Army during the Civil War, was lauded as "one of the most prominent citizens Bell County (Texas) ever had. He was active in all matters that were for the good of the county." His funeral was attended by "one of the largest (crowds) ever gathered around a grave in Belton and was in a way an imitation of the high esteem and love in which he was held."

Jo Zach Miller, Jr. (seated at desk) with customers inside the Belton National Bank where Miller got his start in banking as the bank's manager.

Today, the Joseph Miller home in Belton, Texas, is listed with the Texas Historical Commission, recognized for its unique architecture. According to the Commission, the house, built in 1895, is "one of the largest and most expansively detailed dwellings built during the peak cotton boom years."

Although Joseph remained the Belton bank's president until his death, Jo Zach became involved in the operation of several Texas banks, at one point reportedly holding stock in more than 100. Like his uncle, he also had varied business interests. An advertisement regularly appearing in *The Galveston Daily News* in the early 1890s listed Jo Zach Miller, Jr., among the agents for the Royal Insurance Company of Liverpool.

After nearly three decades in Texas banking and business, Jo Zach left the Lone Star State for Kansas City where he began work as vice president of the Commerce Trust Company in 1910.

The family was so well-respected in the Belton area that rumors of Jo Zach, and possibly other Miller family members, heading north prompted an article in the July 12, 1910 edition of *The Bell County Democrat* headlined "Millers to go to Kansas City." Texas newspapers later followed the early stages of Jo Zach's career in Kansas City, with one writing about him again in 1911.

"He is well-known as a conservative, safe and reliable banker all over Texas," the newspaper wrote. "His many friends in Bell County and Texas are pleased to see him forging to the front in Kansas City and predict that within a short time he will be one of the leading bankers in that section of the West."

The Miller family ranch in Texas. Jo Zach Miller, Jr., later said he was at the ranch when he received word that he had been chosen as chairman of the Federal Reserve Bank of Kansas City.

KANSAS CITY

After four years at Commerce, Miller found himself selected to be the first chairman of the Federal Reserve Bank of Kansas City. He was visiting the family ranch in Texas when he received the news, which, he would later say, caught him unprepared.

In a transcript of the first meeting of new Federal Reserve Bank of Kansas City's Board of Directors, Miller says he received a telegram from Commerce Chairman William T. Kemper back in Kansas City indicating a wire had been received at the bank from Washington inquiring if Miller would accept the post with the Federal Reserve. Kemper and E.F. Swinney, former president of the American Bankers Association and a later adviser to the Federal Reserve Bank of Kansas City, accepted the job on Miller's behalf before letting Miller know he had been offered the job.

In a later interview, Miller showed a sense of humor in explaining how he arrived at the job.

"The governing board in Washington … (sent) the wire to Kansas City and some of my banker friends here did the damage," Miller told the reporter. "That's all I know about it."

"Kansas City is highly pleased at the appointment of Mr. Miller."

Despite Miller's apparent surprise, his selection was praised locally and welcomed in the banking community, which was nearly unanimous in its support.

"Kansas City is highly pleased at the appointment of Mr. Miller," reads one newspaper account. "He is regarded as an excellent choice for this very important place and it is gratifying that he can see his way clear to accept the responsibility."

The paper went on to note that taking the job meant Miller would have to surrender all of his personal investments in financial institutions, which the paper called "a lifetime of financial activity" for a man "rated at more than a millionaire."

Comparatively, his starting annual salary at the Federal Reserve would be a mere $7,500.

"Only a worthy desire to be of patriotic service can justify such a sacrifice," the newspaper said. "And the people of District number 10 are fortunate for having such a man available for this service."

The Federal Reserve

In a 2006 interview, Jo Zach's grandson, Jim Miller, said his grandfather likely felt a sense of duty about the job and probably did not consider the historical significance of what he was doing.

"Duty was a great thing to him," Jim Miller said. "I think he had a job to do. I don't think there was any historical grandeur connected to that job at all — it was a job that had to be done."

Initially it wasn't clear what, exactly, that job was.

Miller was appointed as the Bank's first chairman, a position from which he hired the Bank's first employees and led the Bank's Board of Directors through the hectic days leading to its 1914 opening. With the Bank operational, however, it quickly became clear that Miller was better suited to serve not as the Bank's chairman, but its governor – the position that is today the Bank president.

The governor's position "required someone of both large banking experience and resourcefulness and executive ability," Jess Worley wrote in an unpublished history of the Bank. On Jan. 4, 1916, the Board voted to name Miller to the governor's post while Charles M. Sawyer, a former Kansas Bank Commissioner who had been named the Bank's first governor, would replace Miller as chairman.

At the same meeting, the directors also authorized paying Miller $15,000 annually for his new position, but Miller rejected the increase and, at a Feb. 24 meeting, his governor's salary was lowered to $10,000. In 1917, the directors tried again to raise Miller's salary to $15,000 annually, but he asked for the

Jo Zach Miller, Jr., in the lobby of the Federal Reserve Bank of Kansas City building at 925 Grand on opening day.

Jo Zach Miller, Jr., sits for a portrait by French artist Charles Bennell. The portrait was unveiled in April 1922, shortly before Miller's retirement. It now hangs in the Federal Reserve Bank of Kansas City's headquarters at 1 Memorial Drive.

matter to be reconsidered and "materially reduced." They eventually settled on $12,500.

In return for those relatively minimal sums, the Federal Reserve received a full day's work. And then some.

"He worked all the time," grandson Jim Miller said. "He was up early in the morning, generally around 5:30, and he would start working."

An edition of a local newspaper gossip column that included items about several local bankers said Miller was "the first to work in the morning and the last to leave at night. He has more fun working on holidays than any other time."

Miller's strong work ethic started while he was a young man working at the bank in Belton, when a visiting banker from Waco, Texas, told Miller about the benefits of long hours.

Miller recounted the man's words for an article published in the May 17, 1925 edition of *The Kansas City Star*:

"Providence has so shaped things that any man working eight hours a day can make a living for himself in the state in which he is existing at that time. The ninth hour he works, however, is all profit to him, because there is no overhead to it. The same applies, also, to the tenth hour – the eleventh – and the twelfth," Miller said.

"He has more fun working on *Holidays* than any other time."

The long days were troubling to Miller's doctors, who believed he was in poor health. His father's death had been attributed to weak lungs and physicians were convinced Miller would also die young, likely younger than his father. Their predictions were based in part on Miller's small frame.

At the age of 19, he weighed a scant 116 pounds. Doctors ordered exercise and time outdoors, but Miller resisted, his only workout being the block walk between his home and the bank. By the age of 30 – an age well beyond what the doctors expected him to reach – Miller weighed 145 pounds and said he felt fit. At the time he turned 62, he claimed he'd never spent more than 24 hours in bed with any illness.

"The doctors were rather wrong about me," he told *The Star's* reporter for the 1925 article.

THE GOVERNOR

Miller regularly traveled throughout the Tenth Federal Reserve District and had a strong connection to the community bankers, likely because of his own background in Texas banks.

"It's like a field commander, you've fought the insurgents … you know how they work and it's the same way. You know what the economic demands of these small towns and bankers are," said Miller's grandson, who followed his grandfather and father into banking.

"He knew all the banks. He was well-known in the banking field."

These visits to banks would occasionally involve Miller helping to transport cash between the commercial financial institutions and the Federal Reserve.

According to one newspaper account, Miller once carried $2 million worth of gold certificates in an envelope as he walked the streets of Kansas City, prompting a secretary to ask if he realized the risk.

"Nobody knew I had it, and besides, I look like a farmer," Miller says in the newspaper account. "If I had told a crook I had money, he wouldn't have believed me."

It's unlikely that Miller did look like a farmer. He was well-known for wearing a dark suit and bow tie daily. A 1948 story in *The Kansas City Star* about Miller's 85th birthday noted that the bow tie had been "a 70-year habit."

He tried to break that habit only once, sporting a bright red necktie to the family breakfast table one morning. The tie "astonished" his family, an Associated Press reporter wrote in a May 1942 story, forcing Miller to rethink his decision. By the time he left for work, the familiar bow tie had returned and the necktie was not seen again.

The bow tie is in evidence in a mural of Miller painted by Charles Benell, a French artist who painted portraits of many prominent Kansas Citians in the early 1900s. The portrait has been displayed in the Bank for decades.

"He always had the same suit," his grandson said. "He had a black bow tie … and a coat and trousers that matched. And high shoes. He always wore high shoes."

Other things well-known about Miller were that he was his own bookkeeper, writing numbers so small a magnifying glass was necessary to read them, and that he did not drive an automobile, instead taking the streetcar to work. A photograph accompanying a 1942 Associated Press article featured Miller riding the street car.

Automobiles, he believed, were an "absolute unnecessary extravagance."

"The one thing I never could condone is the way our supposedly better class citizens think their whole day will be spoiled if they don't motor downtown to work each morning," he told a reporter.

Other than his watch chain, the only jewelry he ever wore was a signet ring that he donned annually on his birthday – a gift from his mother when he turned 50.

MOVING ON

Of all his traits, however, Miller was best known for his dedication to his job and the willingness to work long hours. His work ethic was so well-known, in fact, that word he was considering a vacation prompted speculation in the financial community of his possible resignation.

"Kansas City bankers said the gossip started when Governor Miller visited local steamship agents inquiring about rates and bookings for European passage for himself and family," *The Kansas City Post* reported in its June 13, 1922 edition. "It is known that the governor has had no vacation since coming to Kansas City."

The speculation proved true as Miller submitted his resignation to the Bank's Board of Directors just a week later on June 22, 1922.

Coverage in *The Kansas City Star* praised Miller's leadership.

"Executive direction of the federal Bank in this District has been a strenuous task, first in the rapid

A map of the Tenth Federal Reserve District hangs behind Jo Zach Miller, Jr., in a photo that was believed to have been taken on April 16, 1921, in the Bank's offices inside the R.A. Long Building. The floral arrangements were likely in recognition of the corner-stone ceremony at the 925 Grand building, which was held that day. Interestingly, Miller also turned 58 on the same day.

expansion of the Bank's functions in the war period and later in the credit stress that came as a war aftermath," *The Star* wrote, going on to praise Miller for maintaining a "firm grasp on the District's financial situation" during a period of financial stress.

Miller was specifically lauded for developing a "progressive discount rate," which placed a penalty on excessive borrowing but kept the average rate below discount rates elsewhere. It was seen as a method of distributing credit equitably while curtailing inflation.

Among the other accolades was a letter from W.P.G. Harding of the Board of Governors of the Federal Reserve System, saying he was "surprised and disturbed" to learn of Miller's planned departure.

"I am glad to know that at last you are going to take a rest and that you will spend a few months in Europe with your family," Harding wrote. "You have done … monumental work for the Federal Reserve System and I have often wondered what kind of a constitution you had in order to keep on the job almost from dawn to dark all these years that you have."

"I am happy to leave the Kansas City Federal Reserve Bank in *Capable* hands."

His last day at the Bank was July 1, 1922. Employees wished him a tearful farewell during a brief ceremony where he was presented with a silver tea service set. It was one of the first events held in the new Bank building's auditorium, coming a mere seven months after the facility opened for business.

"I am happy to leave the Kansas City Federal Reserve Bank in capable hands," Miller said in the July 4, 1922 edition of *The Kansas City Star*. "And very happy, indeed, to leave the 500 federal Bank employees housed in healthy and pleasant working quarters in the new building."

Worley's written history reflects the idea that Miller felt like he had been able to give the Bank a firm foundation on which to build its future.

"When the Bank became properly housed in the new building and the various departments were working harmoniously and with adequate room and working facilities, Governor Miller's greatest ambition was achieved, and he began looking forward to a vacation of which he had deprived himself during his connection with the Bank," Worley wrote.

Later years

Miller's "vacation" in Europe would likely not meet the standard definition of a break from work.

As he was departing, he told a reporter from *The Kansas City Star* that he was going to spend his time overseas "studying commercial activity and seeking something of the foreign viewpoint. I never took a vacation just to get away from a desk."

Upon his return to the United States, Miller was hardly retired, becoming what *The Kansas City Star* called "a sort of financial doctor." He was involved with several endeavors related primarily to helping struggling businesses, including a bondholders committee working to save the Long-Bell Lumber Company and the reorganization of the W.S. Dickey Clay Manufacturing Company. He was also active in the Kansas City Kaw Valley and Western Railroad.

In interviews after leaving the Bank, he regularly told reporters that success was the result of three elements: concentration, close application and determination.

"If a man makes use of each of those to the utmost, then adds to them the practice of economy and the habit of making conservative investments, there is no reason on earth why he should not make a conspicuous success of his life."

After battling a lengthy illness, including a 13-month stay in St. Mary's Hospital, Miller died at age 87 on Feb. 16, 1951. A *Kansas City Times* editorial published on Feb. 19, 1951, called Miller "one of the salty characters of Kansas City.

"An intense individualist, a man of deceptively modest appearance, but of immense force, where 'J.Z.' sat was the head of the table."

Miller, the editorial said, "was of the hardy pioneer type that laid the foundations for American progress. The West, in which his lot was cast, profited greatly from the shrewd independence of men like him who for so many years kept the nation's economy on an even keel."

Miller was preceded in death by his wife, Mary Elizabeth, in 1943. He is buried in Belton, Texas.

Jo Zach Miller, Jr., in his later years, still wearing the bow tie and dark suit for which he was well-known.

WILLIS JOSHUA BAILEY, GOVERNOR, 1922-1932

Willis J. Bailey may be the only man who was referred to as "the governor" before holding that position at the Federal Reserve Bank of Kansas City.

Bailey was born Oct. 12, 1854, in Mount Carmel, Ill. After graduating from the University of Illinois, he considered studying law at Harvard, but instead came to northeast Kansas to begin farming land owned by his father. He started what would become a large livestock feeding operation and later founded the town Baileyville on his property. He became active in politics and was elected to the first of two terms in the Kansas legislature in 1888. In 1893, he became president of the Republican State League.

His first documented interest in banking was the organization of the Baileyville State Bank in 1895. In 1896, he ran for Congress but lost to his political rival Charles Curtis, who would later serve as vice president under Herbert Hoover. Bailey was elected to an at-large Congressional seat two years later in 1898 and served one term. In "A Standard History of Kansas and Kansans," William E. Connelley writes that at the end of the Congressional term, Bailey "retired from public life to his ranch in Nemaha County."

The retirement, however, was short-lived. In 1902, Bailey was elected Kansas' 16th governor.

During his tenure, he dealt with the aftermath of the 1903 Kaw River flood and saw the completion of construction on the Kansas state capital. His tenure, however, started with what, at that time, was a small controversy generating headlines nationwide: Bailey, who was in his late 40s, was a bachelor.

"The people of Kansas believe it is not good for man to be alone, particularly as there are in Kansas so many bright and pretty girls, who, with reasonable and proper wooing, would make good wives" reads a newspaper account from the *Portsmouth (N.H.) Herald*.

The article goes on to say that Kansans were especially concerned because they had spent $70,000 on a governor's mansion that had been used by only Bailey's predecessor, Gov. William Stanley.

"The people of the Sunflower State are exceedingly proud of the executive mansion and do not propose to have it occupied as a bachelor's hall," the article said. "Society of the state looks upon

Willis Bailey had a lengthy political career in Kansas before coming to the Federal Reserve Bank of Kansas City. He served terms in the state's legislature, as governor and in Congress.

the mansion as a place for its annual ball and other social functions and matrons demand that the governor … install a wife as mistress in the house."

A story in *The St. Louis Globe-Democrat* attributed Bailey's bachelorhood to being jilted by a woman he had met while a student at the University of Illinois. Bailey had been engaged to the woman, who remained at the university when he left for Kansas.

"For a while the correspondence was voluminous, the tenor of the girl's letters being all pleas for him to return. Then school opened, and the rival appeared," the newspaper said.

Bailey received a letter from the woman ending the relationship and, soon after, an announcement of her marriage.

Shortly after taking office, the controversy ended when Bailey married Ida B. Weede, a saleswoman at a Kansas City store who newspaper accounts called "a sweetheart of his youth." A wedding reception held at the Kansas state capital is among the more notable social events in Kansas history.

The Federal Reserve

Shortly after leaving the governor's office, Bailey moved to Atchison, Kan., and became managing officer and vice president of the Exchange National Bank. He became bank president in 1916.

He also was involved with other banks and businesses and served as president of the Kansas Bankers Association during the period when the Reserve Bank Organizing Committee was considering locations for the regional Reserve Banks. Under Bailey's leadership, the KBA asked its 1,145 members to sign petition cards supporting Kansas City, Mo., as a site for one of the Banks – 1,008 responded favorably.

Later in 1914, Bailey was elected to the first Board of Directors of the Federal Reserve Bank of Kansas City. The Board chose him to serve as governor after Jo Zach Miller, Jr., resigned in 1922.

"Language is inadequate for me to express to you the sincere appreciation that I feel for the great honor you have just done me in making me the governor of this Bank, and having come to me unsolicited, intensifies that feeling," Bailey told the directors upon his selection.

As head of the Federal Reserve Bank of Kansas City, Bailey often referred to the Tenth District as "the bread basket of the world." *The Kansas City Star's* coverage of his death gave the account of a meeting Bailey once attended in New York where participants were talking about earnings from securities investments. Bailey told them that the earnings were actually only changes in bookkeeping and that "out in the Tenth District we brought $3 billion in new wealth from the soil last year."

Bailey was also involved in what is perhaps one of the most bizarre incidents in the history of commercial banking.

According to a story in the Dec. 5, 1926 edition of *The Los Angeles Times,* numerous depositors in Kansas City's Park National Bank received anonymous phone calls warning the bank was about to fail and they should immediately withdraw their deposits. About 100 customers, including some who had already written checks for the balances of their accounts, lined up outside the bank before opening.

"As the doors of the building were opened the crowd turned and saw the armored truck of the Tenth Federal Reserve Bank pull up at the curb and guards take their position to guard cargo.

"This bank is as Sound as any of its size in the city."

"The display was nicely timed and the crowd was forced to make way for the guards as they carried the bulging sacks of silver and gold into the bank, together with the large packages of currency," reads *The Times'* account. The crowd followed the guards into the bank where they were greeted, according to *The Times,* "by three smiling girls handing out carnations. Many of the men in the crowd recalled attending bank openings and obtaining flowers, but none ever heard of an institution of finance passing out favors at what appeared to be its doomsday."

Bailey then stepped to the front of the group, introduced himself and yelled to the crowd that he pledged "the millions of the Federal Reserve if you stop this run. This bank is as sound as any of its size in the city."

The run was averted and the few individuals who had managed to withdraw their accounts in the opening minutes of the day returned the funds as deposits.

Although the Federal Reserve played a role in averting the run, most of the credit went to the flowers.

"The carnations saved the day," one of the bank's directors told the Los Angeles newspaper.

LATER YEARS

Bailey had the "opportunity to humanize" the Federal Reserve as its governor, *The Kansas City Star* said in a Jan. 7, 1932 article about the appointment of his successor, George Henry Hamilton.

"Gov. Bailey took a broad leadership and human understanding to the position," *The Star* said. "He knew Tenth District bankers and the customers (in) back of them."

The final years of Bailey's term were marked by illness. His health began to fail after a double mastoid operation and continued to deteriorate. Federal Reserve memos from 1929 indicate that he occasionally was unable to come into the Bank and was kept abreast of Bank developments while at his home. He was granted a 60-day leave of absence in early 1929 and spent at least part of the time recovering in California.

Continuing health problems forced Bailey into retirement in January 1932. He had hoped to travel with his wife after retiring, saying that for the first time in 56 years he would be free to go and do what he pleased.

"I am not wealthy, as they measure wealth in Kansas City, but I have enough to spend these last remaining years in comfort and travel," he told *The Kansas City Star* as his retirement began. "It is one of the comforts of age that it inures one to the final passing of life. If I had been told at 40 that I had but 10 more years, I would have been disturbed, tremendously disturbed. Now I face the probabilities with calmness and find great satisfaction in my reflections."

Willis Bailey (right) at the cornerstone ceremony for the Federal Reserve Bank of Kansas City's Oklahoma City Branch building, which opened in 1923.

The Bank's directors presented him with a silver vase and passed a resolution recognizing his service.

The remaining months of Bailey's life were difficult, and later newspaper accounts said he was bedridden for several weeks.

He died May 19, 1932, at age 77. His funeral was attended by numerous bankers, including some who had been involved in the effort to win the regional Reserve Bank. Among the 47 honorary pallbearers at his funeral were George Hamilton, his successor, and H.G. Leedy, who would eventually succeed Hamilton at the Bank's helm.

Bailey is buried in Atchison, Kan.

GEORGE HENRY HAMILTON, GOVERNOR/PRESIDENT, 1932-1941

George Henry Hamilton had much in common with his predecessor at the helm of the Federal Reserve Bank of Kansas City. Both were Kansas bankers, both held elective office and both were Illinois natives. But while Willis J. Bailey was able to serve as the Bank's governor until failing health forced his retirement at the age of 77, new regulations mandated Hamilton's retirement despite the efforts of the Bank's Board of Directors and area bankers, who hoped he could serve longer.

George Hamilton was a Wichita banker before his selection as governor of the Federal Reserve Bank of Kansas City.

Hamilton was born April 4, 1875, on a farm near Wellington, Ill. His father, John Hamilton, was a successful farmer with land in both Illinois and Texas, and an elected official holding several county offices before serving in the Illinois legislature.

George Hamilton graduated from Olivet College and did postgraduate work at both Harvard and Northwestern Law School. He was admitted to the Illinois Bar in 1901, and in 1903, entered banking at the First National Bank in Watseka, Ill. He was appointed the bank's president in 1910. Following in the footsteps of his father, Hamilton successfully ran for a seat in the Illinois legislature in 1906 and was re-elected to two additional terms. He was one in a crowded field of nine candidates vying to serve as state House speaker in 1909.

"Hamilton is recognized as honest and capable and, at the same time, he is not a wild-eyed radical," an unnamed source told

The Chicago Tribune for a Dec. 13, 1908 story.

Hamilton's bid to lead the House was unsuccessful.

He left Illinois for Kansas in 1912 after purchasing the State Savings Bank in Wichita. He served as its president until a merger with Fourth National Bank in June 1922. The merger came as Hamilton was returning to politics with an election to the Wichita City Commission in 1921. He served on the commission for three years, including a year as the city's mayor in 1922.

He was also becoming increasingly active in the banking industry. In 1929, as vice president of the Fourth National Bank, he was a featured speaker at the American Bankers Association's annual meeting where he was among those calling for change in national bank laws, which he said gave unfair advantage to state-chartered banks. In his comments, Hamilton said regulations were leading national banks to surrender their charters in large numbers. Since national banks are required to be members of the Federal Reserve System while state banks are not, Hamilton argued that the dwindling number of national banks presented a grave danger to the stability of the nation's central bank.

> *"Hamilton is recognized as Honest and capable and, at the same time, he is not a wild-eyed radical."*

Shortly after the address, Hamilton was named president of Fourth National Bank.

The Federal Reserve

The Board of Directors of the Federal Reserve Bank of Kansas City unanimously elected Hamilton as Bailey's successor on Jan. 7, 1932.

"The Tenth District directors have used exacting care in canvassing for a man of strong character and comprehensive experience to take the governorship at one of the important periods in the Bank's usefulness," *The Kansas City Star* said, with a reference to a struggling national economy that was in the midst of what would be known as the Great Depression.

As 1932 drew to a close, with President Herbert Hoover serving the final lame-duck months of his presidency, the nation's banking situation deteriorated with a series of bank failures as depositors demanded their deposits in gold instead of Federal Reserve notes. The bank runs pushed gold reserves under the legal limit at the Federal Reserve Bank of New York. Commercial banks in 37 states were either closed or operating with restrictions on withdrawals.

"Eggs were thrown at the door of the Bank and people were outside Begging for money."

As Franklin D. Roosevelt took office, he faced the challenge of restoring the nation's confidence in its banks. A little more than 24 hours after the inaugural address where he famously proclaimed "the only thing we have to fear is fear itself," the new president ordered the immediate suspension of all banking activity, declaring a banking holiday. The order, issued at 1 a.m. on Monday, March 6, was designed to give Congress time to provide a solution to the worsening banking crisis. The Emergency Banking Relief Act was passed on March 9, 1933.

Some insight on what the bank holiday meant for the Federal Reserve was offered in a 1996 written submission to the Federal Reserve Bank of Kansas City's archives by James H. Joyce, a long-time employee of the Bank's Denver Branch.

"It was like an automobile going 60 miles an hour and applying the brakes, and putting everything in reverse," Joyce wrote. "Checks had to be returned and notices of non-payment had to be mailed out, and everyone in the Bank worked well into each night."

Joyce said that with the constant flow of information in and out of the Bank, a Bank official ended up spending the night on a sofa in the telegraph operator's office.

"It was real chaos because there was no way to cash a check. Eggs were thrown at the door of the Bank and people were outside begging for money," he wrote.

"I think this was the only time in my life that I had doubts that the sun would rise the next day. Bankers were coming into the Fed with suitcases of collateral. I thought it was the end of the world, but it was not, and the banks eventually opened up."

On March 13, the first bank reopenings were allowed for member banks in Federal Reserve cities. Banks in clearinghouse cities were scheduled for opening the following day, and rural banks the day after that. In the Kansas City metropolitan area, the schedule meant that while Kansas City, Mo.

banks were open on March 13, Kansas City, Kan. banks did not open until the 14th, and suburban banks, classified as "country banks," did not open until the 15th.

Although there were some instances where the reopening process dragged on for weeks, 2,488 Tenth District banks were open without restrictions on March 15, 1933, according to an Associated Press story issued that day. An additional 226 banks were open with restrictions and 134 remained closed. As was the case nationally, the Associated Press article indicated that much of the banking business involved deposits with few withdrawals. Hamilton told the Associated Press reporter that many Tenth District banks had, in fact, canceled previously ordered currency shipments they apparently thought they would need on hand if a large number of customers came to demand their money.

George Hamilton's performance at the helm of the Federal Reserve Bank of Kansas City during the 1933 banking holiday was praised by the local media.

The Kansas City Star coverage of the reopening in the paper's March 13, 1933 edition said there was "a flood of money" moving into the banks.

"With a buoyancy of spirit that matched the exhilaration of the early spring morning, Kansas City went to its 24 reopened banks this morning," *The Star* wrote in an article that went on to note one commercial bank sent $5 million in excess currency, which it had held through the holiday, back to the Federal Reserve.

Reflecting on the year, the Federal Reserve Bank of Kansas City's 1933 annual report says the bank reopenings were "orderly … and without any recurrence of deposit withdrawals. Subsequent developments have been generally helpful to the banking industry, including energetic and constructive efforts to rehabilitate banks not permitted to reopen after the banking holiday and to strengthen the position of all banks not possessed of ample unimpaired capital structure."

Hamilton's work during the bank holiday was recalled in an article published in the Feb. 28, 1941 edition of *The Kansas City Star,* which said the Bank's leader "appeared to advantage as a calm, level-headed executive, intent on a program constructive for this area."

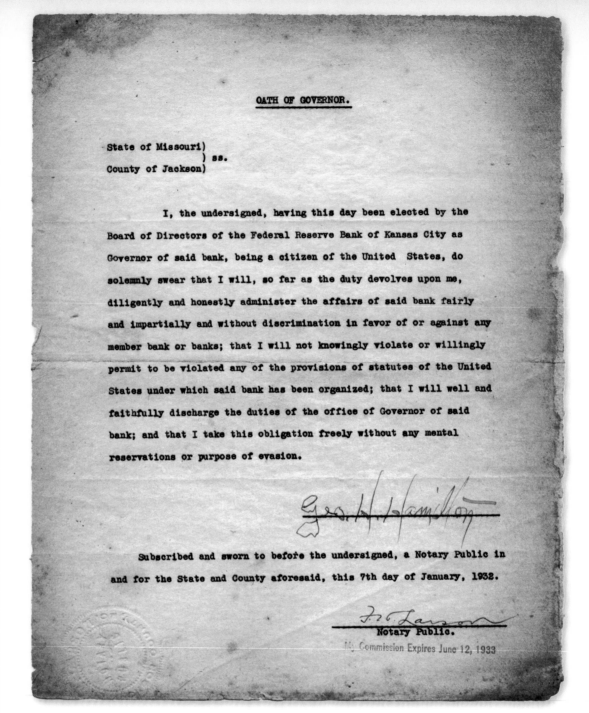

The Oath of Governor signed by George Hamilton in 1932. Only a few years later in 1935, legislation changed Hamilton's job title to "president." Other changes included mandatory retirement.

THE PRESIDENCY

Congress passed two additional pieces of legislation to address concerns about the nation's banks during Hamilton's tenure. The Banking Act of 1933 and the Banking Act of 1935 made numerous changes to the nation's financial infrastructure, creating the Federal Deposit Insurance Corporation (FDIC) and making significant changes within the Federal Reserve, including the establishment of the Federal Reserve's Federal Open Market Committee.

The 1935 legislation also changed Hamilton's job title, making the former Bank "governor" into a "president," who was appointed to a five-year term by the Bank's Board of Directors, with the approval of the Board of Governors of the Federal Reserve System. The act also replaced what had been a full-time job as chairman and Federal Reserve agent with a part-time chairman of the Bank's Board of Directors.

Hamilton's retirement also was the result of changing regulations. Under rules imposed during his term, Federal Reserve Bank presidents could not be reappointed to another five-year term if they would reach age 70 during that term. Hamilton, who was 66 when his term ended on Feb. 28, 1941, was forced to retire.

According to the "It Happened in Kansas City" column in the Feb. 9, 1941 edition of *The Kansas City Star,* Hamilton had the backing of the Bank's Board of Directors, as well as District bankers.

"The Tenth District committee went to Washington with the suggestion either that the Kansas City election be on a year-to-year basis or that Mr. Hamilton commit himself to resigning on his 70th birthday," *The Star* said. But the Board of Governors "held this would be adverse to an orderly handling of the Bank appointments in the 12 Districts."

Both Hamilton and C.A. Worthington, who had been the Bank's second in command since 1919, retired on Feb. 28, 1941.

"…I feel I got More out of the Bank than the Bank got out of me."

Directors, officers and employees presented Hamilton with a movie camera and projector, and gave Worthington a portable radio and a still camera as retirement gifts.

"These have been interesting, happy years of work," Hamilton told *The Kansas City Star* in an article published the day of his departure. "It has been sufficiently different from commercial banking to constitute a liberal education. Considering this, and a broadened acquaintance, I feel I got more out of the Bank than the Bank got out of me."

He returned to Wichita and served again as vice president of Fourth National Bank. He died after a brief illness on Jan. 19, 1948, at the age of 72.

"He was one of the most widely known bankers in this section of the country and had a great civic interest in the growth and welfare of Wichita," *The Wichita Eagle* said in its Jan. 19, 1948 story about his death.

Hamilton is interred in the Old Mission mausoleum in Wichita.

HAROLD GAVIN LEEDY, PRESIDENT, 1941-1961

Harold Gavin Leedy's selection as president of the Federal Reserve Bank of Kansas City on Aug. 28, 1941, ended a six-month period where the Bank had no president – at that time the longest such gap at any of the regional Reserve Banks – and started what would turn out to be the longest tenure of any of the Kansas City Bank's presidents.

Harold Gavin Leedy, who went by his middle name, was raised in rural Missouri and obtained his degree from William Jewell College.

Leedy, who went by his middle name, was born Dec. 6, 1892, in the small southern Missouri town of Benton. His father, Charles, was a storekeeper known as "Judge Leedy" by the community for his work on the probate court. His mother, Laura, a housewife, was the daughter of a steamboat captain who had once employed a young Samuel Clemens, later more widely known by his pen name, Mark Twain.

Much of Leedy's life was captured in a biographical sketch featured in the 1952 book "Leaders in Our Town," by Kansas Citian Richard B. Fowler.

According to the book, when Leedy was 12, the family moved north to Cameron, Mo., hoping that leaving the swampy area around their south Missouri home would improve his mother's health. In Cameron, the family owned the Cameron House Hotel, and Charles Leedy became the county probate judge.

Gavin attended William Jewell College, where he was nicknamed "Shotgun" for his booming voice, but was forced to return home midway through his senior year because of his mother's illness. After working briefly as a clerk in the Missouri Legislature, Gavin obtained his degree from William Jewell in 1915. He went to Kansas City in 1916 where he worked for attorney James E. Goodrich, the son of Cameron banker N.S. Goodrich.

James Goodrich specialized in banking law, working primarily for Commerce Trust Company. However, the Federal Reserve Bank of Kansas City, which had opened only a year earlier, was among his other clients.

"An Enemy artillery barrage opened, and he leaped into a shell hole."

While working for Goodrich, Leedy attended law school in Kansas City. His education, however, was interrupted again, this time by war.

Leedy served in France in World War I after being a member of the first graduating class at the Officers' Candidate School at Fort Riley, Kan., in 1917. He served for about a year before an injury resulted in his return to the States.

"One night … he was caught on reconnaissance in no man's land," Fowler writes. "An enemy artillery barrage opened, and he leaped into a shell hole. The hernia he acquired that night led to his return to the United States. An Army hospital operation followed, but too late for further action."

Leedy was among a group of American military officers lauded as heroes on their return to the United States in October 1918. He was one of about 30 veterans honored at a luncheon in New York City, and he was included in a photograph of several soldiers in the Oct. 18, 1918 edition of *The Washington Post* under the headline "Pershing Officers Return With Tales of Heroism of Americans."

Once back in Kansas City and at the Goodrich law office, Leedy immediately met the woman he would later marry, Goodrich's secretary, Elva Liter.

According to Fowler, the couple's first date involved a film after dinner at a popular downtown Kansas City restaurant called the Tea Cup Inn. The Tea Cup Inn operated for many years in the Glendale Building on the northeast corner of 10th Street and Grand Avenue – the site that would later house the 21-story headquarters of the Federal Reserve Bank of Kansas City. Although the restaurant relocated to the other side of Grand Avenue in the spring of 1919, it is possible the couple's first date was, in fact, on the site that would later be home to the Bank's headquarters.

A year after returning home from war, Leedy graduated from the Kansas City Law School and began to work more extensively in the field of banking law. He also taught night classes on commercial paper at the school for several years. Among his students was future President Harry Truman, who, after leaving the White House, would lease office space in the Federal Reserve Bank building while Leedy was the Bank's president.

THE BANK'S LAWYER

Goodrich dissolved the law firm to become vice president and general counsel for the Commerce Trust Company. Leedy, who had established a reputation as an expert in banking and financial law, decided to open his own office in leased space in the Federal Reserve Bank of Kansas City headquarters at 925 Grand. Fowler writes that because of Leedy's strong reputation, the Federal Reserve Bank of Kansas City became one of his many clients.

He became increasingly involved in banking in the years that followed.

"The deluge of bank business came with the bank failures of the 1930s," Fowler writes. "Leedy was a lawyer-doctor constantly being called to the bedsides of sick banks. Throughout this part of Missouri, Kansas and Oklahoma, he worked on reorganizations, mergers and liquidations. This was not only legal work but a wide exploration into the fundamentals of banking. He learned the causes of health and illness as a young doctor learns from a clinic and post-mortem operations."

"Leedy was a Lawyer-Doctor constantly being called to the bedsides of sick banks."

In February 1938, he went to work for the Bank full-time as vice president, general counsel and secretary to the Bank's Board of Directors. The move started speculation that Leedy was in line for the Bank's presidency, a position he attained on an interim basis likely earlier than anyone expected.

When Bank President George Hamilton prepared to retire, it was widely expected that C.A.

Worthington, the Bank's second in command and one of its longest-serving employees, would be named the Bank's next president. Worthington, who had joined the Bank in June 1917 as head of the Liberty Bond Department, however, saw his health begin to fail and retired along with Hamilton on Feb. 28, 1941.

The Bank's Board of Directors immediately promoted Leedy to first vice president. Since the Bank had no president, the promotion also made Leedy the temporary head of the Bank. According to an article in the March 1, 1941 edition of *The Kansas City Journal,* the search for Hamilton's permanent successor was expected to be completed in "two or three weeks" with Leedy then returning to his post as first vice president.

It did not happen, and six months later, the 48-year-old Leedy was named president. The Bank also announced the appointment of Henry H. Koppang, an employee of the Board of Governors of the Federal Reserve System, as first vice president.

Little is known about the reasons for the lengthy delay resulting in Leedy's appointment.

Gavin Leedy and his wife Elva Liter at the unveiling of Leedy's presidential portrait.

"Neither representatives of the Bank here nor of the Board in Washington – which has to approve appointments originating here – ever have commented on the reasons for the unusual delay, but the natural supposition has been that Kansas City and Washington found it necessary to iron out a few details," *The Kansas City Times* reported in a Aug. 29, 1941 story announcing Leedy's selection.

The newspaper said that Leedy was always seen as the front-runner for the job, although it was estimated that more than 100 names from throughout the seven states of the Tenth Federal Reserve District "were brought to the Kansas City Board's attention."

Among the congratulations received upon his selection, was a letter from the colonel who had been his commanding officer during the war. According to Fowler, the colonel wrote that Leedy's success had shown the character and qualities he exhibited as a young man had "carried (Leedy) to great success in civil life."

The letter was one of Leedy's most prized possessions.

THE PRESIDENT

Although Leedy's father was nicknamed "Judge" and his brother was chief justice of the Missouri Supreme Court, Bank employees affectionately referred to Gavin Leedy as "Judge."

"The Bank was a real big family, very close, in those years … and Judge Leedy was kind of the head of the family," Wil Billington, retired executive vice president, said during a 2006 interview. "He played the role well.

"He was a very warm person. He had a great deal of loyalty to the people he worked with, and he created an atmosphere of warmth and people wanting to help each other."

During Leedy's 20-year tenure, the Bank continued to expand. Total assets at the time of his retirement in 1961 were $2.3 billion, up from $721 million at the time of his appointment. The Bank's staff had grown similarly, from 600 at the time of his selection to 1,200 when he left the Bank.

He spent considerable time on building programs at the Bank's three Branches, leading an expansion of the Omaha Branch and starting a remodeling project in Oklahoma City.

In a retirement message to employees, Leedy wrote that his years at the Bank "could not have been more satisfying or enjoyable.

"As we all recognize, this is a unique organization we serve," he wrote. "The scope of our Bank's activities as a part of the (Federal Reserve) System is so varied and diverse, it is not always recognized that each and every position in the Bank contributed to the System's great goals. To have been in the center of this complex work all these years has been an experience I would not trade for any other. It has been completely absorbing and exhilarating throughout. I cannot begin to count my blessings."

Leedy died July 28, 1989, at age 96. He is buried in Kansas City's Forest Hills Cemetery.

Gavin Leedy (right) with the two men who followed him in succession to serve as president of the Federal Reserve Bank of Kansas City, George Clay (left) and Roger Guffey (center).

George H. Clay, President, 1961-1976

George H. Clay was the first – and, so far, the only – native of the greater Kansas City area to serve as president of the Federal Reserve Bank of Kansas City. It was a position he came to after already making an important contribution to the city while working for what was another major Kansas City institution: Trans World Airlines.

In addition to his career as an attorney, George Clay was a professional singer and worked closely with Howard Hughes at TWA before coming to the Federal Reserve Bank of Kansas City.

Clay was born Feb. 14, 1911, in Kansas City, Kan., to G. Harry and Linnie Phillips Clay, a pair of Indiana natives who moved to the Kansas City area. George Clay attended elementary schools in Kansas City, Ohio and New Jersey before returning to the Kansas City area and attending Southwest High School the year it opened. He went on to Kansas City Junior College and transferred to William Jewell College in Liberty, Mo., before finally enrolling at the University of Missouri – Columbia, where he earned a law degree.

Before he practiced law, however, he was offered an opportunity to pursue another career path.

While at MU, a music lover offered to pay Clay's way to the Juilliard School of Music to further develop his baritone singing voice. Clay turned down the offer.

"At that time, performers could either make it big and get rich in radio or stay poor and struggling," Clay said in a 1976 interview. "I decided I was more interested in the potential of law as a career for me."

Although he was admitted to the Bar in 1934, he continued to sing professionally. For about five years he earned nearly as much from his performances as he did from his legal work. He gave up the professional singing, he said, after he was introduced once as "an up-and-coming young singer" instead of an "up-and-coming young attorney."

In 1940, he married Harriet Hawley of Kansas City.

He practiced corporate law for 10 years until 1944 when he "went over to TWA to handle a little matter for them and never got away," he told *The Kansas City Times* in 1976.

He joined the airline as its assistant director of state affairs. Eventually, he became TWA's vice president of administrative services and a member of the board of directors. He was widely involved with the airline, working on everything from mail contracts to labor and airport negotiations. Ironically for a man who would later head a Federal Reserve Bank, one of the few areas of the airline with which he had no involvement was finance.

First Vice President Henry O. Koppang (left) and George Clay in a photo from the early 1960s. Koppang served as the Bank's first vice president from 1941 through 1966.

While at TWA, Clay was largely responsible for developing what is now New York City's John F. Kennedy Airport. In Kansas City, he was heavily involved in consolidating TWA's overhaul base from Delaware to Kansas City. The move was a key component in the later expansion of what was then known as Mid-Continent International Airport into Kansas City International.

"It wasn't just my love of Kansas City that prompted me to push for the base here," he told *The Kansas City Times* for a March 4, 1976 story. "Let's face it, Kansas City's location is ideal."

During Clay's tenure at TWA, the airline was owned by the eccentric and reclusive Howard Hughes. Clay's wife later recalled some of her experiences during that period, including trips to meetings of the airline's board of directors with her husband.

"He (Hughes) was a mystery to all of us," Harriet Clay wrote in 1976. "These men were running his airline and none of them had ever seen him.

"We often attended meetings at the Beverly Hills Hotel in Los Angeles or the Beverly Hilton, or in Las Vegas at the Desert Inn. Always, (Hughes) was supposed to be living on the top floor of the hotel and probably would attend the meeting, but he never did."

In the same document, which is now in the Bank's archives, Harriet Clay recalled a late-night phone call her husband received while he was a vice president and member of the airline's board of directors.

"We were asleep in bed and the telephone woke us," she wrote. "When George finished the series of long-distance telephone calls, I looked at the clock and it was 4 a.m. As far as I could gather from hearing only one side of the conversation, it was Howard Hughes and he was leaving Los Angeles right away for Phoenix and he wanted George … to find him a remote private place to stay where no one would know him. … George did it, called him back and we went back to sleep.

"I was curious. George understood or didn't care."

THE FEDERAL RESERVE

Clay left the airline in February 1958, coming to the Federal Reserve Bank of Kansas City as vice president and general counsel after learning about the open position from a friend.

He told a Bank employee publication that he had two reasons for leaving TWA and coming to the Federal Reserve:

"The first was that I felt that everyone should spend some time paying his rent for his place in the world. I thought that the Federal Reserve Bank was … an excellent place to find opportunities for both public service and challenge.

"The other part of my decision was based on the opportunity to maintain a permanent home for my family in Kansas City. I had been traveling up to 5,000 miles a week for TWA, and I had seen the world. Further advancement at TWA would have required a move to New York."

He later said that when he accepted the job at the Bank, he thought there was a good chance he would one day rise to the presidency. Three years after arriving, he was selected the successor

George Clay (far right) was among those breaking ground on the Federal Reserve Bank of Kansas City's Denver Branch. The building at 1020 16th St. opened in 1968. Although the 16th Street Mall area is today a popular destination for both Denver residents and tourists, the background shows a far different neighborhood back then. Others handling shovels during the groundbreaking were Bank Director Cris Dobbins; Ann Love, the wife of Colorado Gov. John Love; and Bank Chairman Homer A. Scott.

to H. Gavin Leedy. Also during the Jan. 19, 1961 meeting where Clay was named president, the Bank's Board of Directors promoted Lyle E. Gramley to official status as a financial economist. Gramley would later become a member of the Board of Governors of the Federal Reserve System in 1980.

During his nearly 15 years as Bank president, Clay was known for his open-door philosophy and his use of wry poetry to make a point. The singing voice that had supplemented his income as a young man led holiday carols annually in the Bank lobby.

"He liked to ask people if they were having Fun."

"When you think of George Clay, you think of a man with an expansive sense of humor," former Bank spokesman Barry Robinson told *The Kansas City Star* for a 1995 story. "He liked to ask people if they were having fun."

During his tenure, the Bank constructed a new Denver Branch office and changes were made to the Bank's management structure. He was also well-known as a strong supporter of the Federal Reserve's decentralized regional system.

The press release announcing his retirement included a lengthy quote on the issue:

"The System's foundation rests firmly in regional orientation which has served the nation well. It's a sound blending of public and private interests focused toward an efficient financial system and the overall health of the nation's economy. Regionally, we have supervisory and operational responsibilities with the banks in our own area. We take regional views to national forums.

"This arrangement permits the System to have a better chance to accomplish objectives through solid policies developed in a free and open manner. This is true for monetary policy, bank regulations, our own operations – every aspect of our activity. These Fed traditions are really closely related to traditions of liberty and freedom of choice we all prize so highly. The Fed is an institution that was well-conceived and generally has been well-administered. I hope its strengths can be preserved while it changes in response to the needs of the nation."

He was deeply involved with numerous civic and charitable organizations in the city, including the United Way, Starlight Theater Association, Kansas City YMCA, and American Royal Livestock and Horse Show.

When he retired in February 1976, Clay was the longest-tenured of the Federal Reserve's 12 regional Bank presidents and the senior member of the monetary policy-setting Federal Open Market Committee.

"The creation of money and credit is a very complicated thing," he said in a 1976 *Kansas City Star*

story. "It's not a science with its rules carved in marble. It's an art. Though it is pretty easy to take the first step in the creation of money and credit, what happens in six months as a result of that step is impossible to predict."

In a farewell interview with the Bank's employee newsletter, he talked about the Bank's staff.

"I've often said that the people of the Federal Reserve Bank of Kansas City have made me look good. The technique of getting good people and putting them to work at important jobs does produce results," he said.

At the time of his retirement, Clay said he planned to continue his charitable work and spend time at a Lake of the Ozarks home, which he designed. In the late 1970s, he was involved in trying to help investors recover funds lost in the collapse of two financial services firms. He was also of counsel for Morris, Larson, King and Stamper, P.C.

He died on Oct. 11, 1995, in his Mission Hills, Kan., home at the age of 84.

The Oct. 9, 1968 meeting of the Federal Reserve's Federal Open Market Committee. George Clay is seated at the far end on the right side of the table. Then-Federal Reserve Chairman William McChesney Martin, Jr., is on the left side of the table in the middle with his elbow resting on his chair. Martin is the longest-serving Federal Reserve chairman, holding the position for 18 years and nine months. Clay (left) was active in numerous Kansas City civic organizations and charities.

J. Roger Guffey, President, 1976-1991

J. Roger Guffey was happily pursuing a career as a partner in a law firm when the Federal Reserve Bank of Kansas City came calling in the late 1960s and put him on a path that would later lead to the Bank's presidency.

Guffey was born Sept. 11, 1929, in Kingston, Mo., a small town about a half-hour northeast of Kansas City. His father was a farmer and rural mail carrier, and his mother was a housewife.

"Those were not easy times," he later said. "As a result of the Depression, people had to essentially fend for themselves, and I think my family probably fell in that category. My upbringing in a farm community during the Depression has had an impact on my thinking about what my contribution to the workforce should be."

In 1952, he received a degree in business administration from the University of Missouri – Columbia. After three years in the Army working with intelligence forces in Germany, he returned to MU where he earned a law degree in 1958 and met his wife, Sara.

"I was Happily doing what I had set out to do."

He was a partner in the Kansas City law firm Fallon, Guffey and Jenkins, a firm he had spent a decade building, when the Bank's Vice President of Supervision Jerry Swords tried to convince him to come to work for the Bank as general counsel.

"I didn't have any interest because I thought I'd be practicing law for the rest of my life," Guffey said in 1991. "I was happily doing what I had set out to do."

That all started to change late one morning at his law office when Guffey's phone rang and the caller asked Guffey if he had any lunch plans. When Guffey said he did not, the caller identified himself as George Clay, president of the Federal Reserve Bank of Kansas City, and invited him to the Bank for lunch.

"I felt kind of trapped, so I did go to lunch," Guffey said. "George was a pretty good salesman. About three months later, I had sold the law practice to my partners."

Clay, he said, convinced him that a couple of years at the Federal Reserve would be helpful to his law practice by giving him a better understanding of banking.

"My concern was that I'd walk through those big doors and I hear them slam behind me one morning and realize that I only had one client and if I didn't like that client, what was I going to do?" Guffey later said.

He started at the Bank as general counsel in 1968. He became senior vice president of the Administrative Services Division in 1973 and on March 1, 1976, became president of the Federal Reserve Bank of Kansas City.

THE 1970S AND '80S

It is perhaps a bit ironic that Guffey, a child of the Great Depression, was at the helm of the Federal Reserve Bank of Kansas City and a member of the Federal Reserve's monetary policy-setting Federal Open Market Committee during the Great Inflation. He also participated in a meeting that is seen as a key moment in Federal Reserve history and the turning point in the FOMC's battle against inflation.

With double-digit inflation and public expectation that inflation would continue to escalate, the FOMC, under the leadership of Chairman Paul Volcker, needed to take dramatic action. At a rare Saturday meeting, on Oct. 6, 1979, the FOMC decided to shift the conduct of its open market operations to a focus on controlling the money supply by reducing bank reserves instead of its traditional targeting of the federal funds rate. It was a move designed to kill inflation, and while it was successful, it was not painful. The resulting jump in interest rates, with the prime rate hitting a record-setting 21.5 percent in December 1980 and remaining above 17 percent for much of 1981, touched off a recession in the months that followed.

Authors Daniel Yergin and Joseph Stanislaw describe the period in their 1998 book "The Commanding Heights, The Battle for the World Economy:"

"Farmers surrounded the Federal Reserve building to protest the high interest rates. Auto dealers sent in coffins with car keys to symbolize vehicles that went unsold because of high interest rates.

Roger Guffey was working as a partner in a law firm when then-Federal Reserve Bank of Kansas City President George Clay convinced him to come to work for the Bank. Just eight years later, Guffey was president.

Although Federal Reserve Bank presidents are perhaps best known as members of the Federal Open Market Committee, their jobs involve a wide range of activities and interaction with the public. Here, Roger Guffey talks with local students about banking and finance.

Volcker himself would read heartbreaking letters that people wrote to him – about how they had saved for years to buy a house for their parents, but now, because of high rates, could not. He was deeply upset by these letters, but he still saw no choice. If inflation were not stamped out, there would be a much greater collapse."

Guffey recalled the 1979 meeting during a later interview.

"I think back on that event as a tough decision," Guffey said in 1991. "There were divergent views as to whether the draconian steps that we would eventually take were necessary and whether the price that thereafter was paid by the nation was worth the effort. I happened to think it was, and I look back upon that with some warmth and the sense that it was a tough decision and it turned out to be the right one. I think it really demonstrates the positive impact the Federal Reserve can have on the nation."

The decision, he said, also showed the importance of an independent central bank.

"There is no way that you could have approved what we did on Oct. 6, 1979, through our Congress," Guffey said. "It's very difficult for elected officials to make those kind of hard decisions. That's the reason I think our form of a central bank is very important and worth preserving. It's worked and it will continue to work."

Jackson Hole *and* a move upstairs

During Guffey's tenure, the Bank started hosting an event that would become an institution.

In 1978, the Bank hosted its first economic policy symposium, "World Agricultural Trade: The Potential for Growth," in Kansas City. After three years with an agricultural focus, the first monetary policy symposium was held in 1982 in Jackson Hole, Wyo. "Monetary Policy Issues in the 1980s" was the first step toward what would become the symposium's standard structure: It was the first attended by a Federal Reserve chairman, and the first to include international central bankers. In the years that followed, the conference grew to become one of the world's most well-known economic conferences, drawing an international audience of central bankers, economists and academics for a discussion on issues facing policymakers around the world. Although the event started under Guffey's tenure, he readily acknowledged the efforts of Director of Research Tom Davis and Public Information Officer Barry Robinson for assisting in its creation and success.

Other major changes during Guffey's presidency included the relocation of executive offices from the building's lobby to the 19th floor.

"We have a very good and Dedicated workforce."

The lobby, which was sometimes called "the Marble Orchard," was isolating, Guffey said, while moving to the 19th floor increased his opportunities to interact with employees, largely because they were all on the elevators together. The lobby was remodeled into a visitors center with educational exhibits and a gallery area that was later named the Roger Guffey Gallery. Today, the theater in the Bank's headquarters at 1 Memorial Drive is named in his honor.

He retired in September 1991.

In a final interview with the Bank's employee newsletter, Guffey said he was most pleased by the experience of working with the Bank's employees.

"We have a very good and dedicated workforce," Guffey said. "Hopefully, part of that is the result of some enlightened personnel policies and a work environment that encourages people to remain at the Bank, do their jobs in a quality fashion and enjoy what they're doing. I happen to believe this Bank is blessed with that environment, and it seems to me that is not always the case in a lot of companies."

One Mem

THE FEDERAL RESERVE

...orial _Drive_

B A N K _of_ K A N S A S C I T Y

Two eagles hand-carved by Alan Tollakson of Emporia, Kan., adorn the front of the Bank headquarters.

*The building at **925 Grand** served the*

Federal Reserve Bank of Kansas City well for almost 80 years.

The structure's 367,000 square feet, almost twice what the Bank needed at the time it moved into the building in 1921, provided ample room to grow in the decades to follow. Bank operations did not fill the entire structure until the early 1970s, when the last of the lease-holding office tenants left the building.

It wasn't long before there was not enough room.

By 1976, with no more available space, some staff was moved into a neighboring building on Grand. The need for additional space continued to increase. In two moves, the first occurring in 2000 and the second coming a year later, the Bank moved several departments into a total of 63,000 square feet of leased office space a few blocks away from the Bank building at One Kansas City Place.

In January 2002, after multiple attempts to acquire neighboring property for the construction of an addition and years of internal planning, Bank officials announced work was under way on a project to construct a new headquarters.

After considering multiple sites, Bank officials chose the site of the former

St. Mary's Hospital

near Penn Valley Park as the location for

the Bank's new headquarters in spring 2003.

Although the hospital had been vacant in recent years, it was once an important provider of medical care in the city's core.

The Sisters of St. Mary, who had served Kansas City's German Hospital for nearly a decade, opened St. Mary's Hospital in May 1909. The four-story building contained 250 beds, including 72 designated free to serve the needy. The hospital later added a nursing school and dorm. The building's entrance, originally located along Main Street, was moved to an area near the present-day Bank entrance after an addition was made to the hospital's north side.

After years of declining patient numbers, St. Mary's was sold to neighboring Trinity Lutheran Hospital in 1988. The hospital eventually became part of Health Midwest, which closed the facility in 2001.

Today, the Bank recognizes the site's heritage with a memorial built from bricks that were part of the hospital chapel and featuring the chapel bell. The hospital's cornerstone was set into the monument on Oct. 3, 2007, 100 years from the date it was placed for the hospital. A plaque on the monument dedicates it to the Sisters of St. Mary.

The hospital is not the site's only connection to the region's history. The property was part of the Santa Fe Trail and was once owned by Milton Jameson Payne, Kansas City's fourth mayor. Payne, who was known as the "father of public improvements," served six terms in office in the mid-1800s and was only 26 at the start of his first term. He is among the prominent early Kansas Citians buried in Union Cemetery, located a few blocks east of the Bank.

THIS CORNER STONE

OCT 3 A.D 190

Those visiting the ***Bank headquarters*** *enter from Memorial Drive into the Bank's lobby.*

There, visitors have an opportunity to tour a 3,000-square-foot visitors center featuring the Money Museum, exhibits on the history and structure of the Federal Reserve, and view into the Bank's vault. Visitors also may recognize the brass seal that was previously located in the lobby floor at 925 Grand.

The lobby also offers a spectacular view of nearby Liberty Memorial, home to the National World War I Museum.

Architect Henry N. Cobb said the relationship with the Memorial is an important part of the building's design.

"The main challenge was how best to shape the building so it would have the institutional presence it should have and at the same time acknowledge the Liberty Memorial," Cobb told *The Kansas City Star* for a Nov. 16, 2004 story.

The architect described the building's office tower and the structure's distinctive curve as deferring to the memorial.

Cobb, who is a founding partner of the firm Pei Cobb Freed & Partners, has designed several landmark buildings in his long career, including Boston's John Hancock Tower, the U.S. Bank Tower in Los Angeles and the National Constitution Center in Philadelphia, among many others.

Local architectural work was done by Ellerbe Becket.

At the time of the move, the Federal Reserve Bank of Kansas City building at 925 Grand was the oldest *Federal Reserve* structure still in use.

The 1 Memorial Drive building offers the Federal Reserve Bank of Kansas City about 600,000 square feet of office space – almost twice what was available to the Bank at 925 Grand.

Of the nearly 75 firms involved in the project as contractors, suppliers and consultants, more than 60 were businesses based in the seven states of the Tenth Federal Reserve District. Notably, limestone used on the building was from Cottonwood Falls, Kan.

J.E. Dunn Construction, established in 1924, was the construction manager for the project. The firm is the largest commercial contractor in the Kansas City area. Among its local projects are the Sprint World Headquarters in Overland Park, Kan., and the Charles Evans Whittaker United States Courthouse in Kansas City, Mo.

Construction on the building started with a groundbreaking on June 6, 2005.

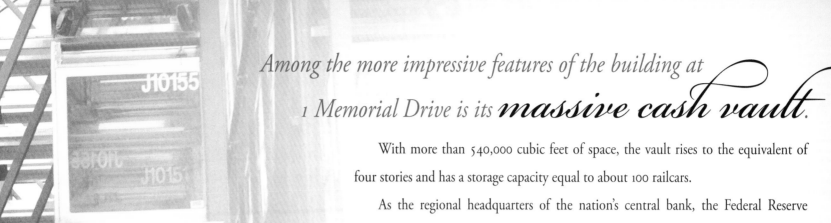

Among the more impressive features of the building at 1 Memorial Drive is its ***massive cash vault***.

With more than 540,000 cubic feet of space, the vault rises to the equivalent of four stories and has a storage capacity equal to about 100 railcars.

As the regional headquarters of the nation's central bank, the Federal Reserve provides currency and coin to financial institutions. Additionally, the Federal Reserve serves as a bank for banks and is the government's bank. The Bank is also responsible for the supervision and regulation of commercial banks and bank holding companies and participates in setting national monetary policy. These missions can be grouped into three large categories: monetary policy, supervision and risk management, and financial and treasury services. Each jet of water in the fountain near the Bank's entrance represents one of these mission areas.

To carry out its work, the Bank has approximately 1,000 Kansas City employees with more than 300 additional employees carrying out many of these same responsibilities at the Bank's Branches in Denver, Oklahoma City and Omaha.

Spanning a region that encompasses the Rocky Mountains,
the Great Plains and the Missouri River, the

Tenth Federal Reserve District

is home to a wide range of business and industry.

From technology and manufacturing to farms and ranches, the District's economy is as diverse as its geography.

The Bank recognizes its tie to the region by flying the flags of each of the Tenth District states in front of the building's entrance. Flags are arranged from east to west in the order of their admittance to the union. The flags were raised outside the building's front entrance – signifying the first group of employees had moved into the structure – on Feb. 19, 2008.

The entrance also features two 16-foot tall bronze sculptures by artist Tuck Langland that symbolize the Bank's long history in Kansas City. The Spirit of Industry, located to the east, and the Spirit of Commerce, on the west, are three-dimensional representations of the relief sculptures that were created in 1921 for the front of the Bank's previous headquarters at 925 Grand Blvd.

FEDERAL RESERVE BANK *of* KANSAS CITY GROUNDBREAKING

JUNE 6, 2005

THOMAS M. HOENIG

President

To begin this ceremony I want to thank several groups and individuals for joining us here today. As you can see by looking out to the horizon, we have a breathtaking site to build on for the future, and I want to thank those who are making this possible.

First, I wish to thank our employees, who are working in offices scattered around the downtown area. They do outstanding work and with the completion of this building, will be brought back together in one location. I certainly want to thank our Board of Directors for its support. I want to thank our friends at MainCor, especially Clara Vaughn, and Union Hill, especially Kathy Burke, who have been so helpful and supportive as we have prepared for today's groundbreaking.

As part of this ceremony, I ask your indulgence to provide a little history to the presence of this Reserve Bank in Kansas City and why we have chosen to build a state-of-the-art facility now.

Nine decades ago, the Federal Reserve Bank of Kansas City was established as part of a system of 12 banks across the United States. It was chartered as a separate, regional institution because those who created it understood that the strength of our nation's money and banking system would best be preserved if it were not concentrated in any one region or in a select few regions of the United States. As one of the designers noted at the time, the "administration of the Federal Reserve System must be divided between the government, the member banks, and the commercial and broad community interests, in a manner which will safeguard against individual, sectional, or political combination."

As president of the Federal Reserve Bank of Kansas City, I am sometimes asked, "Do we really need regional reserve banks?" I answer, always, that anyone who has a sense of financial and political history, or appreciates the dangers of concentrated power, financial or otherwise, can only answer with a resounding "yes."

We 12 banks are more than an historical accident, we are part of our nation's long history of establishing institutions within a framework of proper checks and balances.

The Federal Reserve Bank of Kansas City was opened in 1914. Just as importantly for today's celebration, our current home at Tenth Street and Grand Boulevard was completed and occupied in 1921, over eight decades ago. At its opening, it was a facility for the times and would serve Kansas City and the Federal Reserve Bank extremely well for much of those eight decades.

But the Federal Reserve Bank of Kansas City, like the economy itself, is a dynamic institution, and has changed. These changes now require that the facilities that house us be significantly enhanced.

Since we occupied our completed building in 1921, the nation's payments system has changed from paper based to more electronics. And our role as banker to the Treasury has changed to a whole different level. Our Bank is part of this payments system committed to ensuring its integrity and reliability through any set of circumstances. But to do this as we must, we require state-of-the-art facilities.

After clearing the former hospital site, construction on the Federal Reserve Bank of Kansas City's headquarters started in 2005.

June 6, 2005

Our discount and lending activities function differently today than they did in 1914. Our supervision of financial institutions and our research, as it involves our knowledge of the regional, national and, now, the global economy, is much more intense and requires enormously more complicated technology. And, of course, our role in monetary policy, in many ways, is more substantial today than it was then.

And finally, we live in a different world as it involves security. The world in 1914 was on its way to war, yes, but not within our borders, not like today. We have a whole new requirement if we are to ensure the financial integrity for Kansas City and around the country.

While our current facility is beautiful, it is unable to meet today's needs. So, here we are at this spectacular location, ready to begin the construction of a new building, which when completed, will provide us a world-class facility; one that will enable us to remain a vibrant part of our 12-bank system for at least the next 80 years.

"...to Serve Our Nation, this great city of Kansas City, and the other great cities and towns in the heart of America..."

It is my expectation that upon its completion, we will be prepared to serve our nation, this great city of Kansas City, and the other great cities and towns in the heart of America that define the Tenth Federal Reserve District.

Credits

Many sources provided information for this book. The dates and names of the source publications are included within the text where they are known. The majority of the cited articles and documents were available through the following sources:

....

The archives of the Federal Reserve Bank of Kansas City;

The unfinished manuscript of the history of the Federal Reserve Bank of Kansas City
by Jess Worley, circa 1922;

The Miller family scrapbooks compiled by Mary Mellor Miller;

The Kansas City Missouri Public Library;

The Mid-Continent Public Library;

The Denver Public Library;

The Omaha Public Library;

The Kansas Historical Society;

The Nebraska Historical Society;

The Oklahoma Historical Society;

The Oklahoma History Center;

The Albert Schoenberg Papers at the Jackson County, Missouri Historical Society;

The Western Historical Manuscripts Collection;

The Harry S. Truman Library;

The Woodrow Wilson Presidential Library;

The National Archives;

The Kansas City Star archives.

The data about Kansas City business and industry in 1913 comes from Kansas City's presentation to the Reserve Bank Organizing Committee.

....

Comments made during the Jan. 23, 1914 presentation to the Reserve Bank Organizing Committee in Kansas City, as well as details of the Committee's visit, appeared in the Jan. 24, 1914 edition of *The Kansas City Times*, the Jan. 23 and 24, 1914 editions of *The Kansas City Post* and the Jan. 24, 1914 edition of *The Kansas City Journal*.

....

Many of the comments made during the Jan. 26, 1914 presentation to the Reserve Bank Organizing Committee in Denver appeared in the Jan. 27, 1914 edition of *The Kansas City Times*, the Jan. 26 and 27, 1914 editions of *The Rocky Mountain News* and the Jan 26, 1914 edition of *The Denver Post*.

....

The comments from the Feb. 4, 1914 Reserve Bank Organizing Committee hearing in Los Angeles appeared in that day's edition of *The Los Angeles Times*.

....

Comments made in the Jan. 20, 1914 Reserve Bank Organizing Committee hearing in Chicago appeared in the Jan. 21, 1914 edition of *The Omaha Daily Bee*.

....

Some of the information about Harry Truman came from notes compiled during a 1996 gathering of former employees to discuss the Bank's history.

....

Some of the information about Robert Owen was published in an article by historian Wyatt W. Belcher that appeared in the fourth edition of the Oklahoma Historical Society's Chronicles of Oklahoma in 1953.

....

Additional information about Robert Owen came from an interview of Dr. Kenny Brown by the author and a production crew from KCPT in the summer of 2007.

....

The research compiled in producing this volume has been placed
in the archives of the Federal Reserve Bank of Kansas City.

Photo credits

Photographs and illustrations are from the following sources.

ABBREVIATIONS:

DM: The Bostwick-Frohardt Collection, owned by KMTV and on permanent loan to the
                Durham Western Heritage Museum, Omaha, Neb.

FRBKC: The Archives of the Federal Reserve Bank of Kansas City

HSTPL: Harry S. Truman Presidential Museum and Library, Independence, Mo.

KCPL: Missouri Valley Special Collections, Kansas City Public Library, Kansas City, Mo.

KSHS: Kansas State Historical Society

LOC: Library of Congress, Prints & Photographs Division

NWW1M: National World War I Museum, Kansas City, Mo.

SHSM: State Historical Society of Missouri

WSCHM: Wichita-Sedgwick County Historical Museum

W&AP: Wilborn & Associates Photographers

WWPL: Woodrow Wilson Presidential Library, Staunton, Va.

....

All other images from the Public Affairs Department of the Federal Reserve Bank of Kansas City.

....

COVER.   FRBKC, Sept. 26, 1922

1.   FRBKC

2.,-3.   FRBKC, photo by Casey McKinley

4.   Scott Indermaur Photography

6.   FRBKC, photo by Anderson KC, Nov. 16, 1921

8.   FRBKC, photo by Anderson KC, May 23, 1920

10.   FRBKC, photo by Casey McKinley

12.   LOC, image LC-USZ62-51391, March 4, 1913

13.   LOC, image LC-USZ62-20570, circa 1913

14.   LOC, image LC-USZ62-37416, circa 1907

15.   *The Daily Oklahoman*, Aug. 22, 1919

16.   LOC, image LC-H261-3378, photo by Harris & Ewing, 1913

17.   LOC, image LC-DIG-npcaa-01044, photo by National Photo Company, circa 1918

19.   WWPL (both)

20.   KCPL, photo by PhotoView, Co., 1880

22.   WWPL

25.   LOC, image LC-USZ62-102727

26.,-27.   *The Kansas City Journal*, April 3, 1914

28.   Image courtesy of Dewitt Henry

29.   LOC, image LC-USZ62-132191, photo by Miss. Reineke, Mar. 27, 1911

30.   KCPL, 1910

30-31.   LOC, image 6a07278, photo by W.H. Jones, 1909

31.   FRBKC, postcard published by Hall Brothers, Kansas City, Mo., 1922

32.   LOC, image LC-DIG-ggbain-15209, photo by Bain News Service

35.   SHSM, The Kansas City Post, Jan. 23, 1914

36.   FRBKC, 1914

37.   KCPL, photo from "Men of Affairs in Greater Kansas City," 1912

38.   FRBKC, postcard published by Hall Brothers, Kansas City, Mo., 1915

40.   *The Omaha Daily Bee*, Jan. 27, 1914

42.   *The Omaha World-Herald*, Dec. 27, 1913

43.   LOC, image LC-DIG-ggbain-13554, photo by Bain News Service

44.   top: LOC, image LC-USZ62-72965, photo by Miss. Reineke, 1911

        bottom: LOC, image LC-USZ62-115124, circa 1910

47.   FRBKC, 1914

48.   KCPL, photo from "Men of Affairs in Greater Kansas City," 1912

50.   right: KCPL, photo from "Kansas City and Its 100 Foremost Men," 1924

        left: *The Kansas City Times*, April 3, 1914

51.   KCPL

53. FRBKC

54. FRBKC

55. FRBKC, *The Kansas City Star*, Nov. 16, 1914

56. FRBKC

57. FRBKC

58. FRBKC, postcard published by Fred Harvey

59. FRBKC, 1914

60. NWW1M

61. FRBKC, photo by Lawrence Fischer

62. FRBKC, photo by Gary Barber

63. FRBKC, *The Kansas City Star*, Nov. 16, 1914 (both)

64. FRBKC, *The Kansas City Star*, Nov. 16, 1914

65. FRBKC

66. FRBKC, photo by Anderson KC, Sept. 21, 1921

69. FRBKC

70. FRBKC, photo by Anderson KC, April 23, 1920

72. KCPL, 1884

73. KCPL, April 24, 1894

74. FRBKC, photo by Anderson KC

77. FRBKC

78. iStockphoto

79. FRBKC, photo by Anderson KC, Nov. 16, 1921

81. KCPL, Oct. 1, 1912

82. FRBKC, circa 1912

83. KCPL

84. KCPL, photo from "Kansas City and Its 100 Foremost Men," 1924

85. FRBKC, photo by Anderson KC, May 17, 1920

88. FRBKC, image from the Mary Mellor Miller Scrapbooks

89.   FRBKC, photo by Anderson KC, Sept. 23, 1920

90-91. FRBKC, all photos by Anderson KC, Oct. 1920-Oct. 1921

92.   top: FRBKC, image from the Mary Mellor Miller Scrapbooks

        bottom: FRBKC, photo by Gary Barber

93.   FRBKC, photos by Casey McKinley

94.   FRBKC, photo by Anderson KC

95.   W&AP, photo by Anderson KC, April 16, 1921

96.   FRBKC

98.   FRBKC

99.   FRBKC, photo by Gary Barber

100.   HSTPL, photo by Harry Barth, circa May, 1954

101.   HSTPL, photo by Harry Barth, circa 1955

102.   HSTPL, photo by Sammie Feeback, circa 1955

103.   FRBKC, photo by Anderson KC

104.   FRBKC

105.   FRBKC

107.   FRBKC, photo by Tyner & Murphy, Kansas City, Mo.

108.   FRBKC, photo by Casey McKinley

111.   Image courtesy of Jim Miller

112.   LOC, image 6a13849, photo by Haines Photo Co., 1914

114.   *The Omaha Daily Bee*, April 1, 1914

115.   DM

116.   LOC, image LC-USZ62-118057, photo by Underwood & Underwood, circa 1910

117.   FRBKC

118.   FRBKC

121.   FRBKC

122.   FRBKC

125.   FRBKC (all)

126-127.	FRBKC, photo by the Commercial Photo Co.
128-129.	FRBKC
130.	FRBKC, photo by Anderson KC, Mar. 24, 1922
132.	FRBKC
134-135.	Images courtesy of Mrs. Ray J. Folks, Jr.
136-139.	Images courtesy of Jim Miller
141.	FRBKC
142.	FRBKC
145.	W&AP, photo by Anderson KC, April 16, 1921
147.	Image courtesy of Jim Miller
148.	KSHS
151.	FRBKC
152.	FRBKC, photo by Blank & Stoller Corp.
155.	WSCHM
156.	FRBKC
158.	FRBKC
161.	FRBKC
162.	FRBKC, April 16, 1961
163.	FRBKC, Oct. 20, 1977
164.	FRBKC, photo by Leo Stern
165.	FRBKC
166.	FRBKC, photo by Mile High Photo, Nov. 21, 1966
168.	FRBKC
169.	FRBKC
171.	FRBKC
172.	FRBKC
174-175.	FRBKC, photo by Gary Barber
176-177.	FRBKC, photo by Gary Barber

178-179.   FRBKC, photo by Gary Barber

180-181.   FRBKC, photo by Gary Barber

182-183.   FRBKC, photo by Gary Barber

184-185.   FRBKC, photo by Gary Barber

186-187.   FRBKC, photo by Gary Barber

188-189.   FRBKC, photos by Lawrence Fischer and Chris Schoenhals

191.   FRBKC, photo by Lawrence Fischer

193.   FRBKC, photo by Gary Barber

208-209.   FRBKC, photo by Anderson KC, circa 1922

Index